LOVE AND SURVIVAL IN BUDAPEST

LOVE AND SURVIVAL IN BUDAPEST

The Memoir of Artur Renyi

Edited by

Ilonka Venier Alexander, Nauszika Mathe-Arvay, and Zsuzsanna Renyi

KARNAC

First published in 2017 by
Karnac Books Ltd
118 Finchley Road
London NW3 5HT

British Library Cataloguing in Publication Data

A C.I.P. for this book is available from the British Library

ISBN-13: 978-1-78220-416-9

Typeset by Medlar Publishing Solutions Pvt Ltd, India

Printed in Great Britain

www.karnacbooks.com

CONTENTS

PREFACE

This memoir, written by Artur Renyi, chronicling his life in Budapest with his wife, Borbala Alexander, daughter of noted Hungarian university professor of philosophy and aesthetics, Dr Bernard Alexander, and sister of acclaimed American psychoanalyst, Dr Franz Alexander, was written retrospectively as a diary. Artur's intent was to give an accurate account of his married life as a gift to his only child, Dr Alfred Renyi, a world famous mathematician who lived through the Nazi invasion of Budapest during the waning days of World War II with his parents. It was never intended to be shared elsewhere outside the immediate family.

The handwritten diary has been in the possession of Dr Zsuzsanna Renyi, Artur's granddaughter (and, hence, Alfred's daughter) and her daughter, Nauszika Mathe-Arvay. In 2013–14, when I was writing the biography of my grandfather, *The Life and Times of Franz Alexander: From Budapest to California*, Nauszika translated several pages of the diary for my research. During some of our discussions, I mentioned to my cousin Nauszika that the diary was compelling and told a story of survival and love that should be shared with the world. During the pre-publication interviews between Dr Brett Kahr and me (prior to the release of my grandfather's biography), elements of the diary were mentioned. It was at this time that Karnac Books agreed to publish Artur's memoir.

Zsuzsi and Nauszika completed the work together, translating Artur's handwritten Hungarian text into English. I then edited the memoir and added historical comments that were lacking but needed in order for the reader to better understand and grasp the full implications of Artur's words. Again, it is important to remember that the recipient for whom this was written was a Hungarian who knew his country's history and who had lived through the dark days of the Nazi occupation of Budapest. There was no need for Artur to elaborate when he wrote these words for his son.

This is, in the end, a love letter from an aging father to his son—an aging father who has just lost the love of his life and wants to make sure their story, her story, is not forgotten. This story just so happens to take place in Budapest, a city invaded by Nazi Germany, near the end World War II. And, Artur and Borka just happen to be Hungarian Jews who are caught up in the occupation. This book defines affection, chivalry, idealism, courage, intellectual questioning, and heartache, and, most important, hope. Hope for not only our family's survival, but for the survival of all of mankind during the twentieth century's worst atrocity, if not in all of human history: the Holocaust.

Artur's wish was that his beloved Borka not be forgotten 100 years after her death. It is now more than ninety years since their fateful meeting when he impulsively asked her to marry him, almost "on the spot", and the beginning of their amazingly profound and moving twenty-seven years together.

My cousins and I present Artur's memoir of the years between 1920 and 1946. It has been a privilege and honor to be associated with this project.

Ilonka Venier Alexander
Nova Scotia

INTRODUCTION

Judit Meszaros

A quarter century—a significant amount of time on a human scale, but infinitesimal from a historical perspective. This is the period covered in Artur Renyi's (1884–1951) memoirs, which he started writing in 1946, with the unexpected death of his wife, in the first moments of grief, in the days before the funeral. He wrote them for his son, Buba or Bubi ("who will read these lines"), to commemorate his wife, Borbala Alexander (1892–1946), Borka, or Mommy, and to soothe the pain of his severe loss.

Their relationship had started out little more than twenty-five years before, in 1920, in a period in Hungary roiling with social tensions, revolutions, and counter-revolutions, when the terror of Regent Miklos Horthy's regime (1920–1944) was well underway and a wave of anti-Semitic hatred was tearing through the country. And in 1946, in a Europe laid waste, their relationship came to an abrupt end with Borka's death. Their personal story is interwoven with that period. Beyond the lives of the two, Artur Renyi's memoirs present the final moments of an educated middle-class existence in the last happy days of peacetime. We are witness to a Jewry once integrated into Hungary's business and culture painfully confronting a political and economic discrimination which would previously have been inconceivable, one which led to

Hungary's anti-Jewish laws prior to World War II (1938 and 1939) and culminated in the Holocaust.

The feelings between Artur and Borka that would deepen into a passionate love and their powerful marital bond represent the central motif of the memoirs. It is from this perspective that we come to see the network of family, friends, and colleagues, and the everyday experience of an assimilated liberal Jewry, with the life of the Alexander/Renyi family in the focus. We also catch glimpses of a few significant episodes from the contemporary literary, cultural, and business worlds, while the presence of psychoanalysis is as noticeable in both their lives as it is in the way of thinking of the educated circles of Budapest.

In this piece of writing that had been intended as a private text, the reader holds an authentic historical document in her or his hands. However, it is necessary to provide some historical context, including the events and main actors, for a clear understanding overall and for a particular grasp of the references in the text, which exceed the limits of the usual footnotes.

The end of World War I (in 1918) saw the collapse of Austria-Hungary. Borders were drawn between the previous member states of the empire, including the border between Austria and Hungary. Hungary grappled with enormous social and economic tensions. In the course of half a year—between autumn 1918 and spring 1919—the country had experienced a liberal, radical revolution (the Aster Revolution of 1918) and two forms of government: the first Republic of Hungary (1918) and the Soviet Republic (1919), which only lasted a few months and had been born of a situation destabilised by the absence of any international support. This situation was exacerbated by the loss of two-thirds of the country's territory through the Treaty of Trianon, which established the peace between Hungary and the victorious Entente powers in 1920. All this was eventually accompanied by a whipping up of anti-Semitism—as has been experienced so often throughout history.

The interwoven histories of the two families

ories of the Renyi and Alexander families are linked f Hungary's nineteenth- and twentieth-century Jewry, ir acceptance to their exclusion and, finally, to their on. A great many assimilated Jewish families in the had Hungarianised their German Jewish-sounding the early twentieth century out of a sense of commit- he nation that had adopted them, and a number of converted to Christianity.

Renyi's family had changed its name from Rosenthal n 1908 and converted to Roman Catholicism. Artur iird of four children born to the union between fac- r and merchant Alfred Rosenthal (1838–1898) and chler (1848–1926). Artur's wife Borbala Alexander) was the fifth child of Bernhard Alexander) and Regina Broessler (1856–1922). Like many ed young women from Jewish families,[4] Borbala hotographer. Her husband Artur was a mechanical training, but his extraordinary feel for languages n to make it through lean times not only by trans- ical texts into Hungarian, but also a number of sig- ks of English literature. For instance, he translated . Wells novels, including *The Invisible Man*. He and one child, Alfred Renyi (1921–1970), Buba or Bubi irs, who became a famous mathematician.[5]

iends and a network of intellectuals

and colleagues in the wide-ranging network in rbala's life are particularly noteworthy. Many of e ranks of the world-renowned great minds of century who had been forced to emigrate from hared the later fate of the intellectuals that had e country. It is thus through the couple's bonds

The memoirs provide a vivid d
whose emblematic ideology featu
concepts *communist* and *Jewish*, anc
became a target of violence brough
lessness. Terror attacks ravaged the
by radical military detachments,[1]
as "the cruelties of Orgovany and
Hungary passed a discriminatory
Act, which restricted the proport
Jewish descent to six per cent. T
launched a wave of emigration i
of scientists, writers, artists, and
country. Many of them would
arts and sciences[2] (for example,
winning physicist, the nuclear
Neumann, who conceived of
photographer Andre Kertesz)
also chose to emigrate;[3] amon
the young generation were M
Rene A. Spitz, and the first s
enc Alexander, who achieve
in Berlin and later in Chicag
hub for these emigres. For e
German language was ine
ernisation and culture, and
and theatres—not to speak
speaking world posed no
generations. At the age of
der, professor of philosoph
garian Academy of Scienc
children, was stripped of
the Academy—and, hum
having held a governme
Republic period. At that
in Switzerland and Gern

The hist
to that c
from the
destructi
country
names in
ment to
them had

Artur
to Renyi
was the t
tory own
Ilona Hirs
(1892–194
(1850–192
emancipat
became a p
engineer b
enabled hi
lating techn
nificant wo
several H. C
his wife had
in the memo

F

The friends
Artur and Bo
them filled t
the twentieth
Hungary or s
remained in t

of friendship that one can grasp the power of the generation of progressive intellectuals whose members included the Pollacsek/Polanyi family with all their far-flung relatives, in particular the famous Polanyi boys who represented progressive thinking and with whom Artur shared friendships; for example, Michael Polanyi, who was a physicist, chemist, and later philosopher, and his brother Adolf, who was an economist. During his emigre years in Berlin, Michael established a workshop with Dennis Gabor, Leo Szilard, and John von Neumann to discuss scholarly issues.[6] We also read numerous stories of humanitarian aid offered by Michael Polanyi, Artur Renyi, and Borbala Alexander. Michael Polanyi supported political refugees his entire life; for instance, he assisted already famous analysts from the Hungarian Psychoanalytical Society, Michael Balint and his wife Alice, in resettling in Manchester in the late 1930s. Later great figures of twentieth-century Hungarian literature, Frigyes Karinthy and Marcell Benedek, were regulars in the Renyis' day-to-day lives. Artur also developed a deep friendship with Gisle Johnson, a Lutheran pastor from Norway, who was living in Budapest and had undertaken a particularly courageous mission in standing up to anti-Semitism there.

As far as psychoanalysis is concerned, Artur's interest in this new perspective and therapeutic method is perhaps best demonstrated by the fact that when he was not even aware that he had fallen in love with Borbala Alexander, he had a dream about an altar and the name "Brokander", a contracted mix of Borka's given name and surname, which carried a deep symbolic message. His friend Adolf Polanyi immediately decoded the first part of the message: Artur wanted to get married. Artur then added the name of the woman of his desires to that thought: Borbala Alexander. This light-hearted little anecdote also demonstrates how psychoanalysis had become incorporated into modern culture and in particular into the way of thinking of the young avant-garde intellectuals of Budapest.

Later, Artur would see individual psychoanalyst Istvan Kulcsar. We also meet a number of analysts in the Budapest School within the family group of friends, among them psychiatrist–psychoanalyst Lilly Hajdu, Borka's best friend, and her husband, paediatrician Miklos Gimes, who later became a candidate psychoanalyst. They established an institute for children in Remetehegy, a hilly section of Budapest which is mentioned several times in the memoirs. This facility was called the Dr Lilly Hajdu Gimes Institute for Special Education and Children's Holiday Resort. Every summer, it became a shared vacation spot for Alfred Renyi and the children of the couple's wide-ranging circle of friends. Perhaps Lilly Hajdu herself was the source of an idea that pointed to the determining role of the unconscious. The idea was that Artur had broken his arm on an outing to "escape the tortures of the firm" for a while, meaning unchecked quantities of text from the managing director to be translated with vague deadlines.

A brief consolidation and then events turn rough

After a brief stint in Berlin, Bernhard Alexander returned to Budapest in 1923. We then gain a glimpse into everyday family experiences through the father-in-law–son-in-law, father–daughter, and grandfather–grandson relationships, and it is not only fascinating examples of a grandson's cognitive development to which we are made privy. We also learn of Borka's tireless efforts towards rehabilitating her father politically. We gain an insight into the family's day-to-day lives, replete with household help, a nursemaid, winter breaks, summer holidays in Hungary, Italy, and Austria, and a great deal of hard work. Owing to Artur's multifaceted talent, noted above, he excelled in a challenging post as supervisor at the Ganz Electric Works and Rail Factory with its 7000 workers and 700 office staff filling both domestic and foreign orders. He translated patent-related texts, technical specifications, letters, and anything else required of him. He capitalised on his knowledge of graphology for a regular newspaper column, and he translated classics of world literature into Hungarian. Aside from their love for each other and for Buba, Artur and Borka's happy and balanced marriage was built on an exceptional sense of commitment. They knew they could count on one another. The full-time job Artur had taken on to provide for his family often encroached on his evenings, while Borka took the arduous task of typing up English texts from her husband's shoulders in addition to her own work as a photographer. Early on, she took pictures of objects and, when she was commissioned, of construction projects as well. Later, she photographed children. Naturally, politics, social tensions, and then turbulent changes all transformed their everyday lives. Interpreting jobs due to emigration in 1938 represented additional opportunities and income, when the Hungarian parliament passed its first anti-Jewish Act a few weeks after the Anschluss, followed soon by a second one.[7] All of this set off a new wave of emigration.

Artur's memoirs offer the reader a film-like experience through his eyewitness accounts of the outbreak of World War II and its escalation, replete with references to contemporary news sources. He reports that the Second World War broke out on 1 September 1939 "with the German–Polish war" (p. 48). Artur speaks of a merely German–Polish conflict, which rapidly takes on the scale of a world war. If I consider the fact that this is not the work of a novelist, but that of a husband mourning his wife—no less than one year after the end of the war—then I realise that anyone who has managed to follow the intrinsic temporal rhythm of events and even resist the temptation to reinterpret them retrospectively is not merely disciplined, but also extremely credible. Artur experienced popular doubt in Hungary that the country could avoid entry into the war. There was also a common disbelief—one which he shared—that the country's leadership and even the majority of its citizens could have an interest in the annihilation of its Jewish citizens. Soon, however, the lives of his own close friends and their family members were at risk. Artur and Borbala did everything within their power to aid them and, indeed, to save them. They engaged in charitable work. One senses that the air was slowly thinning and the tension growing as one event flowed into the next: "My memories of these years are not complete at all" (pp. 51–52).

The relationships between the Renyi siblings—Irma, Oszkar, Artur, and Ervin, from eldest to youngest—were complicated, a situation intensified by the situation of the war. Ervin was forced to flee Hitler's Germany only to return to Hungary with many others because he did not believe the same could happen there. Nor did Artur think it could. With stunned silence, he watched the German occupation of Hungary (in March 1944), a country that was collaborating with the Germans and was thus offering no resistance. He asked, "Where is the army? Where is the regent?" Then, equally stunned, he faced the requirement of wearing the yellow star, which he viewed as a "silly brutality" (p. 57). He was terribly disillusioned. Despite his excellent grades, Buba was only admitted to university on the second go due to his Jewish background. Then he was impressed into the "labour service", that is, forced labour, from which he was fortunate enough to escape. With a "resourcefulness" that was unique in the history of the Holocaust, Jews in Budapest were rounded up in so-called yellow star houses in summer 1944 on orders from the city's mayor—and this was taking place after D-Day, which was, in Churchill's recollection, the beginning of the war's end.[8] The system of yellow star houses meant that Jewish personal and real property was now up for grabs and that the Jews themselves had now been gathered together, "ready for deportation". And this was all being done after the annihilation of the Jews living in the countryside was already complete.

A series of moments, both hopeful and hopeless, followed. Was it possible that international pressure on Horthy would prompt him to put a halt to the deportation of the Budapest

Jews? Was it possible that Hungary would sue for a separate peace? The cost of the regent's political dallying was a coup d'etat on 15 October at the hands of the fascist Arrow Cross party. On 24 November, the government ordered the establishment of the Budapest ghetto. And all this when Rome, Paris, and Brussels, indeed, all of Belgium, had already been liberated and Soviet troops had taken the eastern part of Hungary. There was little doubt that the Germans and their allies would suffer defeat—but the Hungarian fascists carried on their war of robbery[9] and the destruction of the Jews. As Artur Renyi saw it, the "common folk" (p. 60) peopled the Arrow Cross mobs and the gendarmes—those who enforced the government's decrees. Hungary had actively contributed to the Final Solution in providing the seeds for the conception of racism. Borka and Artur were even forced to abandon the family's one-time home. Documents, official requests, special entitlements—these all amounted to nothing. They relied once again on their friendships for protection for the time they remained in hiding. Here we experience all the anomalies of a demoralised country, from baptisms performed assembly line style for astronomical sums of money to the eventual worthlessness of those same baptismal certificates. Surreal situations and improbable stories leap to life from a complex vine of memories. Everything in the world order was stood on its head, and then the opposite of everything might occur. The policeman and pickpocket show compassion and the priest who blesses the sanctuary holds a blasphemous sermon, while Bubi, having escaped the labour service, saves lives with his resourcefulness—including those of his parents.

Liberation—facing reality

Budapest was liberated on 13 February 1945. The city lay in ruins, but every member of this tiny family was still alive. Borka took photographs of Soviet soldiers in a hastily constructed studio, and Artur pitched in as a Russian interpreter. They were paid in lifesaving groceries, beans, flour, and bread, and then a few months later, when Artur began working for the British, money once again appeared as a general medium of exchange—though the pay was minimal. What the three of them earned—after all, Buba was now working as well—was insufficient for them to rebuild their ruined home. This is when Borka turned to the two richest of her five siblings living in America for help: Franz Alexander, who was now a successful analyst, and Lilly, whose husband was a millionaire. Artur provides heartbreaking accounts of how Feri (Franz) had sent a total of twenty-five dollars, half his hourly analyst's fee, and how Lilly had managed to forward fifty dollars on two occasions instead of a hoped-for larger amount. In contrast, Borka's relatively poor elder sister, Erzsi, demonstrated regular care with clothing, money, and packages. Borka was the only one of the siblings who had not emigrated, and, with—according to several accounts—her gentle and giving nature, she stood out the most from her siblings with their rather tough characters. We will never know what had transpired between these siblings, what offences and jealousies had caused this coldness, this lack of love, from which Borka, this "warm-hearted little girl" (p. 76), had suffered—according to her diary. We know from other sources that Borka had been neglected: Ilonka Venier Alexander writes in her book that her grandfather, who is none other than Franz Alexander, never even mentioned that he had a little sister named Borka.[10]

Certainly, that quarter century during which Borka enjoyed her husband's unflinchingly selfless love—indeed, he even saw the world differently in Borka's presence—compensated for this sensitive woman's early lack of love. Artur the grieving husband not only brought Borka and their relationship to life and found consolation in writing his memoirs, but also presents the reader with the opportunity to catch a glimpse of a significant historical period through his personal experiences.

The future

The present time of the memoirs has become a part of the past, but what of the future? Naturally, it was Buba. He got married. He took a young woman named Kato as his bride before his mother's untimely death. They were all full of plans in the hopeful period of the liberation. Buba became a mathematician of international renown; Kato also pursued a university career in mathematics. If the reader experiences the parts of little Buba's life through the memoirs as well as those of the resolute, energetic young man in that family atmosphere that his parents had created, then she or he will not be surprised at how a mathematical genius could also be a hedonist in a positive sense, someone who adores the possibilities life has to offer, who is open to human relationships, who loves doing sports, who has a good sense of humour, and with whom others enjoy spending their time. As a contemporary commented a number of years later, "Renyi was characterised by a Mozart-like lightness and the relish of a bon vivant" (Z. Renyi, as cited by Korner, 2013).

Artur Renyi must have been right when he wrote the following lines about Borbala Alexander: "I am sure she must have been happy herself as well, she who was able to generate so much happiness. She must have been happy … and I must find comfort in this idea" (p. 40). And this happiness clearly also had a great effect on the lives of others.

Translated by Thomas Williams.

Notes

1. Especially cruel mass killings and robberies were associated with a detachment of officers led by Istvan Hejjas. At their court martial in June 1922 the officers defended their actions and said they were following Hejjas's orders. The court martial

declared that Hejjas's actions were "selfless patriotism". In the end, the court cleared the first lieutenant's men of the murder charges and only convicted a few of robbery. Hejjas was granted amnesty by the regent, and the investigation against the detachment was closed, citing Horthy's amnesty order. http://konfliktuskutato.hu/index.php?option=com_content&view=article&id=138:antiszemita-atrocitasok-gyilkossagok-pogromok-a-feherterror-idszakaban-&catid=16:esetek (in Hungarian).

2. Frank, T. (2009). *Double Exile: Migrations of Jewish-Hungarian Professionals through Germany to the United States, 1919–1945*. Bern, Switzerland: Peter Lang.
3. Meszaros, J. (2014). *Ferenczi and Beyond: Exile of the Budapest School and Solidarity in the Psychoanalytic Movement during the Nazi Years*. London: Karnac.
4. http://www.fotomuveszet.net/korabbi_szamok/199734/magyar_noi_fotografusok_a_szazadfordulon?PHPSESSID=2b3c23a4b2c2b105bca2ff7b2ffcefa6 (in Hungarian).
5. Renyi, Z. (2013). *Dialogusok egy matematikusrol* [Dialogues on a Mathematician]. Szeged, Hungary: Szegedi Egyetemi Kiado, Polygon.
6. http://www.polanyi.bme.hu/bio.php (in Hungarian).
7. Act XV of 1938 defined who was a Jew on religious grounds and, based on that, drastically cut the number of Jewish members of professional associations tied to the press, the theatre and film, the law, medicine, and trade to twenty per cent. That same year saw the introduction of a new bill to restrict the "expansion" of Jews in public life and business, which determined Jewish identity based on race in the spirit of Germany's Nuremberg Laws. Passed on 5 May 1939, the second anti-Semitic law banned Jews from the civil service. According to estimates, the first anti-Jewish law directly affected the lives of around 15,000 people in the country, while the second one had an impact on at least 200,000. If one considers the families of

those people, the latter law effectively sealed the fates of over 600,000 people.

8. https://en.wikipedia.org/wiki/Invasion_of_Normandy.
9. On 1 November 1944, the Hungarian prime minister, Ferenc Szalasi, issued a decree that made it possible to confiscate all personal and real property from the Jews.
10. Alexander, I. V. (2015). *The Life and Times of Franz Alexander*. London: Karnac.

Bernard Alexander and Regina Broessler had an apartment on the top floor overlooking the Elizabeth Ring and raised their children there soon after the building opened in the mid-1890s. The building languished in disrepair during Communism and was recently restored and is again a grand hotel reminiscent of its former pageantry. The building was home to the Alexander children and also housed the cafe where Bernard, a philosopher and expert on Shakespeare, sat with students and faculty members discussing aesthetics.]

What actually happened was the following: when I went to study in Vienna at the K.u.K. Graphische Lehr-und Versuchsanstalt [Royal College of Graphics], my dearest mother helped me find a flat. After a long search, we managed to find a more or less suitable room for me at 53 Mariahilfer Strasse [located in the centre of Vienna] and we happily discovered that Margit just so happened to stay in the same house. She married a man from Vienna who worked as the conductor of the Opera Bühnenmusikdirigent [Vienna Stage Music Ensemble]. This fact influenced our choice and finally we picked that flat, thinking I wouldn't be alone in the house since my childhood friend Margit also lived there. And so, we leased the room at once.

Margit was very unhappy in her marriage. Her husband was an untalented musician who was also quite crazy and tortured her with all sorts of follies [psychological mind games]. Margit wanted to obtain a divorce and I encouraged her to do so. Margit told me that an engineer from Budapest often came to see her to court her and wanted to marry her in case she decided to get the divorce. I told her, by all means, she should divorce her husband.

One evening I went to see her and we were chatting. That might have begun around nine o'clock. Her husband usually arrived home from the Opera House at approximately half past ten. When the doorbell rang it was only half past eight.

"Oh, my god," I told her, "is it your husband? Does he arrive today so early?" (Her husband hated me as he knew I encouraged Margit to file for a divorce. For this reason I hoped to avoid meeting him. Additionally, he often expressed his anger towards me in a rude way.) "No, it is not my husband," she answered me. "Certainly it must be that engineer from Budapest who wrote me a letter saying that he would travel to Vienna today and was coming to see me." "Then I am leaving, I do not want to disturb you." I told her this and immediately left for the vestibule. Margit opened the door and at that moment she introduced Artur and me to each other.

At the onset I did not want to accept Artur's offer of this commission because I was about to leave town. I wanted to travel to Munich by boat the next Wednesday evening to visit my dear Father, whom I have not seen for eight months. But this gentleman begged me to take the commission and told me if I did so, I would do him a great favour. Gabor Terey, the director of the Museum of Fine Arts, recommended me to him, and told him that nobody else could take a photo of a piece of art in a creative way but me. This gentleman [Artur] told me he also had to leave the following week, he was to travel abroad as well, and he had to take the photo with him in order to show it to art collectors. The painting belonged to his mother who intended to sell it and he promised to help her do that. He asked me to come to their house on Bimbo Street to offer my services on Sunday morning because he and his mother would be there in the family home.

I reflected that since I was recommended to him by the Museum of Fine Arts, I cannot afford to reject such an offer. I agreed to go there and meet them.

That evening I spent time with some of my lady friends and the friends of my older brother Feri [noted psychoanalyst Dr Franz Alexander]. I talked to them about this unexpected job. Many of them knew Artur Renyi and told me that we would appreciate each other very much.

The next morning was Easter Sunday and I went with my assistant, Rozsi, to their house on Bimbo Street where Artur's mother greeted us. We brought the painting to the terrace, in front of the house, where I took the photo but when I developed it that afternoon it turned out that the exposure failed and consequently I failed to produce a photo. I called them and Artur asked me to go there again on Monday because he needed that photo immediately. That was why I went there again on Monday, this time on my own, without my assistant, and tried a new exposure: I did not take the painting to the terrace but took the photo in the semi-darkness of the hall/lounge, where the painting hung. I used a narrow lens and set the exposure time for half an hour. I managed to take a good photo though it was not quite perfect. (When, after some weeks' time I returned to Bimbo Street as Artur's bride, I took another photo of the same painting and that photo was actually perfect.)

Artur's mother was an especially nice lady of seventy-one years of age but I could sense she was upset that I brought the painting in and out several times; therefore, after finishing the second photo, I told her in German: "Jetzt bin ich schon fertig mit dem Bild, gnädige Frau" [meaning: "I am ready to take the photo, madam"] and she answered me, in not a friendly way: "Na, Gott sei dank,ich hoffe auch, Sie kommen nicht noch einmal" [meaning: "Well, thank God, I also hope you won't come yet again"]. The poor lady must have been disturbed to have the usual procedures of the house turned upside down. She was certainly astonished when I came to the house in a few weeks as Artur's bride and she realised that her wish: "Ich hoffe auch, Sie kommen nicht noch einmal" ["I also hope you won't come yet again"] did not come true. Eventually she grew to like me very much and I would become fond of her. She lived with us for another six years and we never had the slightest difference of opinions. She loved Buba [Hungarian name for baby, the nickname given to Artur and Borka's only child, a son, Alfred] as well.

While I set the exposure for the photo of her painting we talked with Artur and it turned out we had much in common, including some friends, i.e., Misi Polanyi [Mihaly Polanyi, 1891–1976, born as Mihaly Pollacsek, who later, after emigrating to Great Britain used the English first name Michael, was a well-known scholar in the fields of physical chemistry, economics, and philosophy. He was the father of Nobel-prize awardee John Charles Polanyi]. Artur told me he was going to leave for Vienna on Thursday on the so-called Balaton express train. [At that time one had to travel this roundabout route to reach Vienna.] I told him I would also travel by boat to Vienna, on Wednesday evening, and mentioned to him it was a pity we could not travel together and keep each other company. But Artur said he already had organised his trip by train which was to leave on Thursday. We said farewell and I added that I would send the photos to him the following day, and I did.

The following facts I got to know from Artur's version of the story. On Wednesday afternoon Artur was sitting in the office of his lawyer, Dr Karoly Pollacsek, and they were discussing some business. The office was located at 1 Maria-Valeria Street and the office had a clear view to Petofi square from where my ship was boarding. At a quarter to six Artur suddenly decided he would travel by boat and on the very same boat I was taking.

He had not yet prepared to travel and he had no luggage but carried his walking stick. In spite of all that, he called his mother at 5.45 pm to inform her that he had changed his mind and would travel by boat instead of by rail. His mother was surprised as Artur was unprepared and had no luggage with him. He was, nevertheless, totally adamant about his decision. He said goodbye to Karoly Pollacsek, ran down the stairs, and crossed the square towards the boat. He arrived at the harbour at the last moment before the boat's departure, just at the moment before the drawbridge was raised. Artur had rushed onto the boat and in the next moment, it left the dock.

My friends came to the port to say goodbye to me and I waved goodbye to them with my handkerchief. I felt that this myself: "How could I have been so crazy as to agree to marry a stranger?" "Why was it necessary?" But at the same time I felt I could not have done anything else. I felt it was predestined, it was fate. I often asked myself, who wanted it? Today I know the answer: it was Buba [Borka refers to her son, Alfred Renyi, born in March of 1921]. Buba wanted to be born and he made me say yes to this stranger.

The next day I planned to leave for Munich on the 3 pm train. Artur was busy all day but he told me he would bring everything to the station with him that was necessary for the train travel. He promised to arrive at the station before the departure time, if only at the last minute. After I arrived, I waited and waited for what seemed like an eternity before booking a compartment for us. I was afraid he would not come. I imagined that I had daydreamed the entire situation.

Finally Artur did appear, running into the station at 2.57, just three minutes before departure. He caught sight of me and jumped up into the compartment and, again, he was without luggage. He said he did not have time to get it. He embraced me and kissed me and told me he was so busy that he could not manage the time needed to collect his luggage. "It's not a problem," I told him. "But you may not come to meet my Father this way. You should get off the train in Salzburg tomorrow morning and buy all the necessary clothes and other belongings (and I suggested to him a long list of menswear). You can then follow me on the next train to Munich. You can get the information at the Pension Gartenheim about how to get to the Ebenhausen Sanatorium which is where my parents are staying. I will wait for you there."

We agreed to this plan. All night long on the train Artur sang to me. He sang mainly the songs of Schubert, and later he sang many old English love songs. We arrived in Salzburg in the morning and Artur got off the train.

The train was due to arrive in Munich at 1 pm and I expected Daddy to be there waiting at the station for me, as was his usual custom. Daddy loved to meet his loved ones upon their arrival and to be present at their departures. The train arrived right on time but I could not see Daddy anywhere. (Later on it turned out that he misunderstood my telegram, sent from Vienna, and expected me to arrive at 1 am instead.) I was crying and did not know what to do. I thought my sister Magda and her husband, Dr Geza Revesz, were still at the Pension Gartenheim but that was not true. A hotel boy tried to comfort me and told me he would take me to Pension Gartenheim and there I could ask for information about the whereabouts of my sister Magda and her family. The owner informed me that they had already left and could not tell me their new address. I felt alone and I found myself crying again because I knew that Artur would arrive on the evening train and I must talk to Daddy first, before his arrival.

Happily, I met an old lady, Mrs Gero, who lived on the first floor. I asked her to help me find my father without any delay. "Why do you cry?" asked this old woman. "I am engaged to a man who arrives soon and I have to talk to Daddy before he arrives but there is no more train to Ebehausen today," I answered her.

"That's nice," said the old lady. "And who is your fiance?" she asked me.

"I don't know," I answered.

"I am sure you know at least what he is called," replied Mrs Gero.

"Yes, he is called Artur Renyi," was my answer.

"Artur Renyi? He is an old friend of ours. He really is worthy of you! No one will make you as happy as he will. And now we should immediately call your daddy in Ebenhausen," she told me encouragingly.

We called the Sanatorium but we were told Daddy was not there as he had travelled to Munich. My mother answered the phone. "Mommy, Borka speaking. Did Daddy travel to Munich?" I asked her.

"Yes, he travelled there to see you, arriving by the 1 pm train," she answered.

"Where does Daddy stay in Munich?" I asked her in despair.

My mother answered me slowly and patiently: "Well, he certainly cannot be found in the Hotel Regina." However, I was rather impatient and asked her again: "Do not tell me, Mommy, where I cannot find him but instead tell me where I can find him."

"I have no idea," my mother went on to say, "'but he will certainly call Mrs Gero." And that was what happened. Within five minutes' time the phone rang when Daddy called and we agreed to meet at 5 pm in the lounge of the Hotel Regina and have tea together. I was very happy to see him again as we had not been together for eight months. I embraced him and told him immediately: "Daddy, I have to tell you something important. I am engaged."

Daddy was a bit shocked. He sat down, and could only say, "Well, well." I went on and said, "My fiance is not the person you think of," namely my family wanted me to marry B. L. "Who is your fiance then?" he asked me. "Actually I do not know much about him, but Mrs Gero knows him and told me he was a proper gentleman. He is called Artur Renyi and arrives this evening by train and wants to propose officially to me tomorrow," I told him at once.

I went to see Mrs Gero with Daddy and left a message for Artur. We asked Mrs Gero to tell him to get off the train at the station before Ebenhausen and there would be a coach waiting for him to take him into town. Then we travelled to Ebenhausen where I met Mommy. I immediately told her about my engagement and she reacted like this: "Yes, I knew already. You are right,"—apparently, she had the same intuitions and premonitions.

My sister Magda and her husband Geza were there and they had heard something negative about one of Artur's relatives. The next morning we all went to greet Artur who arrived by coach, smiling, and waving his hat. All of us were relieved and thought he could not be a bad man. He was received with love by all of us. Everybody grew to love him. He now had some luggage, including a handbag, but his "wardrobe" was not complete. Magda and I accompanied him to town the following morning to purchase a new hat and an overcoat. The overcoat he had brought with him was purchased at the time of the 1919 Hungarian Revolution and was of a poor quality. I told him to throw it away.

We celebrated our engagement the next evening, on the 12th of April, which was the eve of Daddy's birthday. We had an excellent dinner with cake and wine for our celebration.

Artur wanted to get married right then and there and the others agreed with him. We checked in with the registry office in Ebenhausen to arrange for our wedding and ordered the necessary official documents be sent from Pest. However, before the fourteen days' waiting period ended, all of us received an expulsion order from Bavaria. This was commonplace because of a revolution in Munich and all foreigners were sent home. On Wednesday we received the message along with an order to leave Bavaria within twenty-four hours. On Thursday morning we all left and arrived in Freilassing, located on the border. We were detained because we did not have a valid visa to return to Austria. We were told we had to acquire the visas in Munich. Artur found a railwayman, who travelled to Munich, and who agreed to get the necessary visas and bring them back along with our passports. We booked rooms for the night in a beautiful small hotel in Freilassing where we could leave our luggage. In the afternoon we went to the town to find a goldsmith and ordered our wedding rings. The engravings were completed and the rings were ready to pick up in the afternoon. My ring had Artur's name engraved inside and his had my name. We put on the rings and returned to the hotel. We still had to wait for our passports and so we spent another night in the hotel.

were closer to justice in their poetic language than today's psychoanalysts. Translated to modern thinking it meant that a chance one minute meeting with Borka in Vienna seven years earlier was enough for my unconscious mind to perceive that she was the girl I needed.

But the events of everyday life kept this awareness in my subconscious mind. When I actually realised that I should get married, it took the form of a dream and combined the image and the name in a poetic short form: "Brokander". When I happened to meet Borka Alexander one year later my mind suddenly realised that she was identical to Brokander. Therefore, with the help and stimulation of the gods, I could be brave enough to propose to her, to ask her to marry me, while on the ship. But, I think, I had already been led by the gods when I made that impulsive decision in Pollacsek's office, when I felt the inspiration of an irresistible force, and suddenly changed all my previous travel plans. One may also call it my subconscious mind.

I carefully noted the precise dates. I called Borka on the phone on the 3rd of April, 1920, which was a Saturday. The next day, Sunday, the 4th of April, 1920 was Easter Sunday, and Borka came to see us for the first time on Bimbo Street and the next day, Monday, the 5th of April, she appeared for the second time. On Thursday, the 8th of April, at 10 am I proposed to her and she agreed to be my wife. On the 9th of April, Friday, we left Westbahnhof for Munich. I arrived in Ebenhausen on Sunday, the 11th of April. Our engagement party took place Monday, the 12th of April. On Wednesday, the 14th of April we had to leave. We spent two days in Freilassing: the afternoon of the 14th of April and the morning of the 15th of April. We arrived home in Pest on about the 20th of April. Our wedding took place on the 4th of May, on a Thursday, and we left for our honeymoon, on the Vienna ship, on the 6th of May, on a Saturday.

We got home from our honeymoon about the 20th of May, 1920. This year could be called "the year of preparations" for us.

We called it a year of preparation because that was the year of Borka's pregnancy as we prepared for our son's arrival. We also had to prepare different matters. Namely, we had to arrange our household for our everyday life, we also had to organise our company, and our social contacts, but first of all we had to furnish our home. All of these preparations took place in the middle of the raging counter-revolution, I mean, not at all in a peaceful atmosphere.

It is not necessary to describe the counter-revolution, you [here, Artur addresses Buba, nickname for his son Alfred Renyi, the future reader of his diary] have heard about that. The cruelties of Orgovany and Siofok have already been over. [The White Terror followed the fall of the Soviet Republic after WWI and caused the torture and death of communists and Jews. We can read about these unspeakable atrocities in *Letters from Vienna* by Andor Gabor. Castrations, buryings alive, hangings, mass executions, and other tortures were committed in Orgovany and Siofok.]

This declaration was originally called "The Szeged Idea", but I call it "lack of ideas" because I think it is a stupid, thoughtless concept. The Szeged Idea, also informally known as Szeged fascism, refers to the pro-fascist ideology that developed among anti-communist counter-revolutionaries in Szeged, Hungary in 1919. The Szeged Idea was based upon the claim that Hungary was stabbed in the back in World War I by communists and Jews and was thereby justified to endorse feats to undo this evil by declaring a holy war against such collaborators [Zsuzsanna Ozsvath, Miklos Radnoti, *In the Footsteps of Orpheus: The Life and Times of Miklos Radnoti*, Bloomington, Indiana: Indiana University Press, 2000, p. 8]. Szeged militants promoted Hungarian nationalism, an economic "third way", and advocated a "strong" state. This ideology was based on two different preconceptions. One of them stated the following idea: "All communists are Jewish". This notion was presented mainly to the workers because contemporary politicians wanted to frighten workers and peasants, who have already been influenced by the Church to become anti-Semitic for decades or—one could say—for centuries, and the contemporary politicians based their influence on that (already generated) anti-Semitism.

That was a part of the fight against communism, which, actually, was only a "quasi-fight" as only a very small percentage of the population shared communist ideas and were adherents to the communists of the earlier era because the members of the communist movements did not have that wisdom of the present-day Communist Party's leadership [Artur refers to the Hungarian Communist Party in 1946, which was quite popular at that time]. Former Hungarian communist leaders objected to land reform based on a doctrinaire viewpoint, while carrying out land reform. This can be called the greatest achievement of the present day Hungarian Communist Party.

On the other hand the counter-revolutionary politicians needed such a "quasi-fight", as it was a point of reference—as the Western European plutocracy provided financial support for them—in the form of the Romanian troops marching into Hungary. [This happened in 1919 and Governor Horthy marched in riding a white horse: Artur refers to that event.] Without that support Governor Horthy could not have "triumphantly" ridden in on top of his white horse.

The second statement of the Szeged Idea drew the conclusion, stating … "If every communist is a Jew, then every Jew is a communist". I have to add that before the union of the Communist and the Social Democratic Parties, the Hungarian Communist Party only had a few hundred members. Following a wave of emigration and persecution, the Hungarian Communist Party had fewer than five hundred members, but if we count women and children the party's membership could have been as high as 2,000. Among them were, naturally, the so-called Jews. I think, they were members of an artificially created social stratum. What I mean is, 10 per cent of them practised the Jewish religion, 70 per cent of them were free thinkers, who had only a formal connection to the religious Jewish community, and some of them did not have any connection to the religious Jewish community at all. Another 20 per cent of them were Christian people who had been baptised not such a long time before.

The mathematical and logistical skills of the counter-revolutionary politicians were not sufficient to calculate properly, i.e., assuming 2,000 Communist Party members existed, and 100 per cent of these 2,000 members were of Jewish origin, (and they were not), these counter-revolutionary politicians concluded that "therefore" all of the approximately 800,000 individuals—who were artificially stigmatised as "Jews" by them—had to also be communists. Actually, they should only have concluded that about 25 per cent of them might have been communists. We can state that in reality only 0.25 per cent were communists.

But in spite of all the above data, this second bias, actually a misinterpretation of data, was the favourite conclusion of the many counter-revolutionary politicians. Namely, they based their policy—a policy which wanted to acquire the support of peasants who were afraid of losing their landed property—on the political murders and robberies of Orgovany, and of other places. They also based their ideology on this very same conclusion and started the removal of that part of the population, those who were stigmatised by them as being "Jews". In the beginning these people were removed from universities, from offices, and from positions in intellectual life. They have not been removed from business life yet, but that step was taken later. [Remember, Artur is writing this in retrospect so has the knowledge of future events.]

Grandpa's [Dr Bernard Alexander, father of Borka Alexander and Dr Franz Alexander], position as professor at Budapest Pazmany University was naturally one of the greater targets for attack. How could anybody of Jewish origin keep such a leading position in intellectual life as Bernard Alexander had? He was a professor of philosophy at the University, he was also the editor of a book series, called *Writings in Philosophy*, he was also a member of the Hungarian Academy of Sciences, he was also a writer, a critic, and an author of articles on politics.

He lost his chair at the University, he was excluded from the Academy, he was also dismissed from the journal *Pester Lloyd*, and lastly his telephone line was taken away. I can remember the time when I tried to get his telephone line back for him at the office of the Ministry of Trade, where an employee rejected my request, saying the following: "We will not return the phone line of Bernard Alexander, he is a communist."

Mommy fought this storm for her father with gallant braveness and with endless devotion; qualities that epitomised her character throughout her entire life. It was a very difficult task and a difficult time for all of us. Almost all of Bernard Alexander's former friends abandoned him with the exception of the old Zsolt Beothy [1848–1922, a literary historian], but he was sick in bed and could not help Daddy. Unfortunately, Zsolt Beothy died soon thereafter.

David Angyal [1857–1943, historian and a member of the Hungarian Academy of Sciences] seemed to be well intentioned, but he could not do anything either. Among the professors, Kornis [Kornis Gyula 1885–1958, philosopher, university professor] was the only one who worked actively to help Daddy, which was very nice of him. The Hungarian Academy of Sciences, headed by Berzeviczy, who always called himself a friend of Bernard Alexander, firmly turned a deaf ear to any requests for assistance. Even Jozsef Veszi [1858–1940, writer, journalist, MP], the chief editor of the *Pester Lloyd* journal, was brave enough to call Bernard Alexander several years later, but only when the counter-revolutionary regime had already weakened.

Nevertheless Mommy carried on with her fight, tirelessly and valiantly. Finally, after three years, in 1923 the University reversed their declaration which had removed Bernard Alexander from his chair and reinstated him among the professors. The retirement age in Hungarian society in the years during and after WWI was seventy years of age and Bernard Alexander was then seventy-three. He was obligated to retire though and did receive his full pension because of Borka's tireless work. His pension would equal about 800 koronas in contemporary Hungarian currency.

Achieving these good results would not have been possible without Mommy's ongoing efforts. She also did her best to arrange Pali's [Paul Alexander, Borka's brother] and Geza's [Dr Geza Revesz, husband of Magda Alexander] non-political judicial case. She managed to get the indictments against them dismissed by the public prosecutor's office. Erzsi [Erszebet Alexander, older sister of Borka] also had a judicial case without merit and Mommy also succeeded in getting that case thrown out of court.

In the meantime, we had to struggle to keep our apartment, and to keep the summer house in Godollo [a small resort place near Pest] as well. Later, in 1944, one of the individuals who took part in the political murders of Orgovany, became one of the biggest mass-murderers in world history. Our Godollo villa was claimed by this man as his own and we, therefore, had to fight with him. We finally managed to save the value of the villa for Grandpa even against this evildoer. This in spite of the fact that the deputy sheriff [*szolgabíro* in Hungarian] of that area received everybody with a pitchfork in hand who wanted to buy the estate. According to the requirements stated in Grandpa's will, we transferred the sum obtained for the sold estate to him in Germany in marks. A portion of this sum was spent to cover his costs in Germany, another portion was given to Pali by Grandpa, and the rest of the money was deposited in his own bank account in Germany. Unfortunately, because of the huge German inflation, this amount was worth less than a penny.

We could save the flat in a more indirect way. My right to apply for the flat was approved as I was allowed to apply for it in the name of my limited company as the co-tenant. Another portion of the apartment was let to Dr Klinger and his family. Dr Klinger had an identical twin brother. When I met one of them in the street, I could only distinguish one from the other by asking the following question: "What about business?" If the answer was positive, then he was Pista, our flatmate, who worked as a dentist; if the answer was negative, then it was Gyuri, who worked as a physician specialising in internal medicine.

Anna, their household maid, was already living with us. One day Pista Klinger left the flat at 8 am and half an hour later, at 8.30, Gyuri Klinger arrived, taking his cello with him. He had not been there earlier and he asked Anna: "Does the Klinger family live here?" Anna had no idea about the existence of the twin brother and therefore she thought Dr Klinger had "gone crazy". When Mommy arrived home at noon, Anna told her: "Guess what, madame, Dr Klinger went crazy. Half an hour after he left the flat in the morning he came back home and asked me if the Klinger family lived here. Then he entered the room and played a cello. I stayed in the next room as I did not want to let a madman stay here alone." Poor Pista Klinger and his wife were both killed in 1944.

It was quite a miracle that I was able to avoid political persecution during the counter-revolution. Only a few of my old friends shunned me because they thought me "a communist". But, I was not a communist, just a radical thinker. Following Oszkar Jaszi's [1875–1957, historian and politician] advice in 1919, I accepted some office work in the Foreign Affairs People's Commissar's office. In the autumn of 1919 a political persecution against me began that I could not stop. Later, during the period of our marriage, I did not have any such problems.

The business and economic situations were not easy either though we had to establish a way to earn a living. After Adolf Polanyi left the company, I had to carry out the liquidation of our firm. It appeared to be simple, at least theoretically, as assets were equal to 120,000,000 koronas in contemporary Hungarian currency, and the liabilities were only 1,000,000 koronas. Another 200,000 koronas would cover the cost of liquidation and I could also receive my salary during the period of shutting down. I would organise that, but it was quite a difficult task for me. Some of the liabilities were crucial. For example, if the payment for the equipment were not to be returned, the parties could demand the equipment themselves and, consequently, the debt would have risen to sixty times its original value. Payment in these cases was extremely urgent.

Most of the assets were not "liquid" ones, I mean, they were dissipated among the successor states, therefore I had to arrange this from Vienna. [Due to the Trianon Treaty, the peace agreement to formally end World War I, some territories, which had belonged to Austria-Hungary, were annexed to neighbouring countries, which became the so-called successor states.]

Mommy undertook the task of typing for me so she played an important role in the liquidation process. Later on she managed to type English wonderfully, with perfect spelling, though her knowledge of English was not good enough to understand complicated technological transcripts. However, she played an affectionate, attentive role when I dictated the English texts to her and she tirelessly memorised all sorts of spellings which I explained to her. She did this in such a lively, focussed manner, that was another example of her affection, devotion, and conscientiousness.

Finally, this difficult work of liquidation ended and it worked out well. So well, in fact, that one of the clients returned some equipment and accepted payment in Hungarian koronas (despite their deflated value).

The above-mentioned business transaction could only be accomplished after we applied for a loan from another engineer, which so epitomised the business and financial circumstances of that time period. Though I only needed this credit for a few days, I had to repay almost 50% of my profit as well. It was still worthwhile because in this way I could take further steps in the direction of closing.

Our little boat was swimming on a sea of storms. Maybe the waves could also feel the presence of an angel on board because the storm had suddenly stopped; wherever we went, there was bright sunshine and the stormy sea was calm. As Orpheus tamed wild animals by playing music, Mommy's lovely personality radiated love and demanded respect from savages, or human beasts, who were worse than the wild beasts.

Summer and autumn were fairly uneventful. Sometime, maybe in mid-August, Erzsi invited us to go to Geneva, Switzerland for a fortnight. Grandpa [Bernard Alexander] was also there as he held lectures at Geneva University in French. Erzsi still lived with her first husband, Miklos Gyorgy, at that time. We spent a very pleasant fortnight in Geneva. We did not stay at Erzsi's and they rented a room in a pension for us. We did, however, dine at their place. This was our first chance to spend more time with Grandma [Regina Broessler] after the first few days of our meeting in Ebenhausen. Unfortunately, this so-called longer period was also very short and, in fact, was our last time together as she has already suffered a brain haemorrhage. She was already partly spastic—and a couple of months later she had another stroke. She then had a third stroke and she died in the autumn of 1922 in Badenweiler.

I met Edith, Erzsi's daughter, for the first time during this visit. She was very nice to me; what's more she valued my good talent beyond my merits. We met in Bern as she stayed near there in a boarding school. We applied for some sort of visa in the federal capital of Switzerland. I remember the city hall that had a wide, spiral track leading to the upper level instead of a staircase. We amused ourselves with Mommy, listening to the accent spoken by Swiss people, and we called breakfast "z'nüni" (which actually meant "zu neune") ["nineses"] even after returning to Pest.

When we travelled via Zürich, my English childhood sweetheart, Cissie, came to see us at the railway station, and she stayed there with her husband. Cissie grew fond of Mommy immediately, as everybody did. At that time Mommy showed the first signs of her pregnancy. She wanted to tell Cissie in English that she felt unwell. But instead of saying "I feel very ill" she said *"I feel me very bad"*, as her English was still poor, meaning "I have the impression of being bad". That was quite amusing, as the connection between Mommy and "being bad" was so discordant that it was just amusing. If there was anybody in this world who did not include a spark of "bad", it was her. I do not know anybody who was as near to the perfect, evangelical goodness as she was. Whenever I read the Gospels, I can only think of her. How greatly she was hurt by some of her sisters and brothers, but she returned every wrongdoing with endless love and goodness.

We returned home from Switzerland via Innsbruck, where Mommy did not feel well again, and we interrupted our journey to spend fourteen beautiful, autumn days in Innsbruck. Once we went out for an afternoon tea to a nearby castle where Buba showed his first signs of life. We returned to the hotel in a horse-drawn carriage hired at the castle. We arrived home in Pest by the end of October when an intensive work period began for me.

An important step of the liquidation of the Ganz factory works was the circumstance of the lanolin factory which we established next to the Zsolna broad-cloth factory. Using the invention of Misi Polanyi, we gained back wool fat, which was lost when the wool was being washed in the waves of the River Vag. Then we processed it and produced the finest lanolin. The profit was divided between the company, and Misi, who was also due to receive a share for his invention. We had a row with my business partner, Misi, about a certain sum of money, about approximately 5000 koronas. Our conflict was generated from having different opinions, as I told him that this sum belonged to him, while he said it belonged to me. Finally, we found the solution and invited twelve children living in poverty for a Christmas afternoon tea and gave all of them lovely presents. Mommy organised the entire celebration: she bought the shoes, warm clothes, and underwear, and so on, and she prepared the Kugelhopf and coffee with whipped cream. The children were happy and so was Mommy as she assumed the role of mother and that was so characteristic of her kind-heartedness. This was a perfect and symbolic beginning to her real motherhood.

Afterwards Mommy followed the doctors' advice, to be careful during this phase of her pregnancy, and she spent most of her time in bed. The room that belonged to Grandpa and later to Buba was hers now. Her bed was placed under the window which provided her a good view to Gellert Hill. In the afternoon I usually went for an hour's walk up to Gellert Hill and along the pathway in front of Citadella [a fortress on top of Gellert Hill, on the Buda side of the Danube, built in the nineteenth century by the Hapsburg monarchy]. I lifted my walking stick into the air and drew large circles as semaphore-signals for her. She could see the glitter of the light in the afternoon sunshine. Of course, I could not actually see her, only her window, but I knew she could have seen me and it was good to send her signals. The signals meant I would soon return home to her as being away from her, even for half an hour, was difficult. I could not even imagine that someday the two of us would be split apart from each other by death and my giving signals would be in vain. Well, who knows? I do not believe in what religions teach about immortality and I don't even find them likeable at all; however, I wonder if some unimaginable, some untouchable and inexpressible reality might exist behind all these ideas.

Somehow we got through January and February and, finally, March arrived and we were expecting your delivery around the 20th. And it actually took place then. At the break of dawn on Palm Sunday, 20 March at 3 am, you, my Buba, who would read my lines, arrived into this world.

Some days before your delivery, Mommy moved in to Sanatorium Park and I also followed her on the 19th of March. I got a room on the first floor. Mommy's room was located one floor higher, next to the delivery room. I fell asleep around midnight and was woken at 5 am when your birth (my Buba) was reported to me. I immediately ran into the delivery room. Mommy was lying there, her face glittering with happiness, and you were given a bath. In the meantime you looked at the world like a little wise man and were sucking your finger.

Delivery was quite painful and that is why doctors offered a light dose of pain [the so-called Rausch] medication for Mommy. Nevertheless, she rejected this intervention saying that might hurt her baby, in spite of the doctors' view, who insisted this sort of pain relief was harmless. But Mommy would rather tolerate the terrible pain to avoid even the smallest risk to her baby. Doctors mentioned later with amazement that they had never seen a similar case when someone, having such bad pain, would reject help.

Some days later Mommy and you came home to Franz Joseph [the embankment along the river, in Hungarian Ferenc Jozsef rakpart, today No. 24 Belgrade embankment, in Hungarian Belgrad rakpart]. Mrs Rosenthal, a nurse, came to stay with us and in two weeks Mommy recovered completely and was able to get up. This was followed by the period of breastfeeding. We bought a book about baby-care and we conscientiously recorded your weight gain, every week, as was expected. In the summer we moved into my Mother's house on Bimbo Street, located in Rozsadomb, an elegant garden suburb of Budapest.

I will try to give a description and a characterisation of Mommy but it is difficult for me to find the words. Even the words of the great poets would have been unsuitable to describe her character. Still I will try to present her briefly. First I am going to cite the opinions of some of her closest friends.

Old Aunt Iren said the following: "Sie war die Güte selbst," meaning "She herself personified goodness." Another lady, Dr Lili Rotter, who had a rather cool and objective character, that is why her view can be considered as the lowest: "I have never in my life seen such a combination of selfless goodness and tireless activity. Namely, there are good people who do not hurt anybody, but at the same time they do not do anything for anybody else. On the other hand, there are also active, lively people, but most of them act for themselves. I have never seen that sort of steady activity for other people, for her husband, her son, her father, her mother, her sisters and brothers, and for her fellow creatures in anybody else but in Borka's case."

Yes, that was exactly the very least which could have been told about her, but we can also add something else. Misi Polanyi wrote this to me when he congratulated me on our engagement: "Both of you are still children. Be careful not to have a row as children usually have; in such a case call me and I am going to make peace between you."

Luckily we did not need this sort of peacemaking. Well, we had quarrels, as lovers often do, but it occurred only twice or three times in our entire lives that I let the sun go down upon my anger. And now the light of all my life has died out. [Remember, this memoir is written after Artur's wife Borka died, as a gift to his son, Alfred, known as Buba.] In his recent letter Misi Polanyi wrote: "You have lost the companionship of a lovely soul. Her freshness, humour and kindness as 'a young girl ...'"—yes, these words actually characterise her very well. She was really "a lovely soul", one cannot find anybody similar to her in the entire world. Polanyi was right: she actually personified a flourishing freshness, good spirits, and goodness. Still, all of these adjectives cannot truly characterise the uniqueness of her being.

She was really a child, an unspoiled child. Such a child, about whom Jesus says: Except ye be converted, and become as little children, ye shall not enter into the kingdom of heaven.

Life spoils most of adults. The first step of being spoilt is when as a result of bad experiences we get to be careful and do not show our feelings openly and we become "clever" and diplomatic persons. I myself made the same mistake. She was free from this feature as well. I often was joking with her, saying that her way of talking was a sort of "free association", as she always said immediately what she thought and did not decide if her conversational partner deserves such openness or not. It was quite surprising that her openness never caused her any problems: I think people were so much enchanted by her childish openness that they forgot about taking advantage of the situation.

Getting to know features of her art of photography also reveals her positive characteristics. Once the old Mark Vedres [1870–1961, sculptor] entered her studio and examined a photo that Mommy had taken of one of his sculptures. He exclaimed with surprise, saying: "Well, this photo is even more beautiful than my original sculpture." Naturally, it could not have been better than the original piece, as the photo could only show those features which the original sculpture obviously also had. Mommy's method was the following: first she walked around the statue, before taking a snapshot, trying many angles and many sets of lighting and exposure in order to deeply understand the artist's ideas and to find the best version for her photo. That was why the photo might, indeed, look finer than its subject. This type of observation, which was at the same time artistic and technical, endeavoured to understand the very idea the artist depicted in his work. That was also the way she looked at people as she always managed to catch sight of their best features. This was one of the secrets of her enchanting personality. As soon as somebody felt that he/she was the object of Borka's consideration and focus, they stuck to her, grew to love her, and were able to improve their personalities. At the same time, they were ashamed of their mistakes and would somehow change themselves in order to reflect Mommy's favourable image of them. It seems that in the end she made them better by having scrutinised them.

I am not sure how much I could improve myself and I am not at all satisfied with myself. I am aware of my mistakes, but if I am better now than I was twenty-seven years ago, I owe it all to Mommy. It is she who discovered my good features and qualities and I did my best to be true to the image she formed of me. I do hope and know that this image was not false; these were just the best features I had in addition to my many faults.

Maybe what she saw in me helped me realise my strong wish to be a lifelong and faithful husband to her. I bless my God that she was not disappointed in me. But it was all because of her merits, not mine. Mommy made everyone better. Naturally she could not manage to do so with everybody to the same extent and I refer here to some of her sisters and brothers. Her goodness did not help everybody. I recollect Jesus's words: *Ye may be the children of your Father which is in heaven: for he maketh his sun to rise on the evil and on the good, and sendeth rain on the just and on the unjust. For if ye love them which love you, what reward have ye? Do not even the tax collectors the same? And if ye salute your brethren only, what do ye more than others? Do not even the tax collectors so? Be ye therefore perfect, even as your Father which is in heaven is perfect.*

She was not only good but was brave as well. Her goodness was limitless and obstacles placed in her path did not deter her from offering help to anyone. She did not care about danger. I could list a thousand examples. For example, once she crossed the River Danube at Veroce accompanied only by an old boatman, in a raging hurricane in order to save you, my Buba, and your friends, who were on an island. Spending the night during the storm, without warm clothes and sheets, would have been dangerous for you. Praising Mommy's excursion and her actions could have become the story of an epic poem. She also risked her life, without concern for her safety, when her brothers and sisters needed official documents and she acquired them to save their lives. There were several other occasions when she also imperilled her life for me, for you, for friends, for everyone. Her actions were both good and heroic.

In this chronicle, I have just now reached the beginning of our second year. In those days I was very much involved with my literary work on the Gospels. The first example of my evangelic studies was to write an explanation of *The Sermon on the Mount*. I think it would be right to discuss the main ideas of that study here. I am not led by vanity, just the contrary. This means much more for me as it was a part of that spiritual rebirth I spoke about before, my rebirth represented by my marriage to Mommy and what our life together meant to me.

My study was more like a belief than a scientific essay. It was my first attempt to formulate a worldview which had been crystallised in me for a long time. I am going to introduce its main points here but not in the primitive form of my first essay. I will introduce it in a way to show it has matured since then. Later on I would like to write it in English but who knows whether I will have time for that. Maybe I am going to live long enough to complete it. Now, I am exposing its main ideas here because it belongs to our story.

I would like to begin with a parable. Let us suppose that in 2,000 years from now there would be such a world in which the genre of fiction, novel, drama would have died out, so much so that people never heard of them. Naturally, I am aware of its being an absurd hypothesis; being an absurd assumption. I do refer to it only for the sake of the parable that I would like to explain. On the contrary, in this new world the science of history-writing would have reached a considerably high level, and they would have accurate chronicles, reporting about every significant event and about every important period of past ages. In this new world of scientific history-writing someone would suddenly discover a copy of Shakespeare's *Hamlet*. As these people would not have any idea of the genre of drama, they would certainly regard this piece of writing as a new historical source, just another chronicle of the past, especially one which tells the story of Hamlet, prince of Denmark, whose existence could be familiar for them from the chronicle of Saxo Grammaticus [a medieval Danish historian ca. 1150–1220]. They would identify Hamlet with the Danish prince, living in the ninth century AD. At the same time critical reviews would point out that this writing is totally wrong and incorrect as a historical chronicle. Hamlet would not have been able to attend the University of Wittenberg, because its university was not founded until 500 years later. On the other hand, his country could not enter into war with a Norwegian king, Fortinbras, because such a Norwegian king never existed.

Therefore, in their view, this chronicle should be thrown away as being worthless. Let us suppose that a narrow circle of people, living in this new age, would respect Shakespeare's name without being aware of his actual importance, without having any idea about who he was, and most likely they regarded him as a famous historian. Then these two groups of people would enter into a debate: the smaller group of people would state that the story must be true as it was written by Shakespeare. The opposing group would say that it is evidently wrong and therefore should be thrown away.

It is evident to us that both groups are wrong. In case this story is regarded as a chronicle of events that actually took place, the critics are right to criticise it. Both groups would be wrong to judge the genre if they would interpret it as a historical chronicle, one which tells facts authentically. The first group is wrong. Due to their respect for authority they think that all this happened just as it was written in the drama, and the author was wrong. The second group is right in saying that events could not happen this way, but at the same time they are also wrong by rejecting or throwing away this piece of writing.

We already know that the play Hamlet never aspired to be a precise, historical chronicle. On the contrary, it was written as a drama, a piece of literature, and is one of the greatest dramas in all of world literature. The genre was well known at the time of its origin for both readers and authors, but in that future (at 4000 AD) no one knows that is why both parties are totally wrong.

My conclusion is that mankind has a similar contact to the Gospels. The Gospels represent a genre, which is totally unknown in our time. Nowadays people think that the stories of the Gospels wanted to communicate events that actually took place once, long ago. And, therefore, two circles of viewpoints have been formed. Some critics think that the stories of the Gospels are false because they are obviously contrary to all our knowledge about the rules of Nature. The stories are certainly not true ones. It is impossible to feed 5,000 people by giving them seven loaves of bread and three pieces of fish. Therefore, they conclude that the entire Gospels are false and they do not pay any more attention to them. We have no idea about how to change water into wine just by touching it. But even in the case of someone believing that Jesus was such a superhuman being who can create such a miracle, we can ask the question: what is the point of this sort of miracle?

One group of believers say that all these events took place in spite of their entire incredibility. Naturally, it is against the laws of Nature, but miracles are usually not rational events. Jesus was the son of God, not a human creature who stood above Nature's laws, and that was why he could create miracles and according to them everything happened exactly as it was described in the Gospels. Their interpretation is a literal one.

As for me, I think both groups are wrong. The authors of the Gospels never wanted their readers to believe that these events actually took place. The genre of the Gospels is one that has died out since that time. It is a piece of art, its stories are not chronicles but parables, and by that I mean symbolic stories. The contemporary readers of the Gospels did not need an extra explanation because they were familiar with the genre of parables. Unfortunately, readers of our time do not know or understand this genre any more.

Let's take an example in order to highlight my message. Let's take the example of *the marriage at Cana*. Jesus appears at the wedding. In front of the house, where the wedding takes place, a barrel, full of water is seen. Jesus touches it with his finger and the pure water becomes wine. One of the wedding guests tells Jesus the following words: *"Every man at the beginning does set forth good wine, and when men have well drunk, then that which is worse; but you have kept the good wine until now."*

If we regard this narrative of the chronicle as an event that actually took place, we would just provoke critics. Naturally no one has information on how water can be transformed into wine just by touching it. But even if one believes that Jesus, as a superhuman creature, can work such a miracle, what would be the point of it? One would expect quite a different sort of miracle of the earthly incarnation of God than transforming a barrel of pure water into wine. How should we interpret that Jesus is praised for offering good wine? I think this sort of praise is not at all adequate to the person of Jesus.

The critics are not aware of the fact that the authors of the Gospels did not want to introduce this as a new true story. This narrative is a poetic parable about the relationship of the teachings of Jesus and the Jewish religion. In this narrative the barrel of pure water symbolises the Jewish religion. Jesus just touched it and therefore he radiated his own personality's miracle and that was why it turned to be wine. The above cited comment of the wedding guest is a true, critical view of all religions. Originally every religion was as good as good wine but later people got drunk by drinking it. This can be interpreted in a way that the cheating farmers (here the priests) misused the faith of people to provide them with bad quality wine. This may symbolise the forcing of egoist teachings on religious people, in order to ensure the power of the clergy. Jesus acted in quite a different way: as a result, he appeared 1,000 years after the beginning of the Jewish religion and, therefore, he kept the good wine until the end of the wedding.

The Gospels often include such parables, which the readers of our age can also recognise as parables. When the Gospels say, "*A sower went forth to sow: and when he sowed, some seeds fell by the way side and the fowls came and devoured them up. Some fell upon stony places, where they had not much earth: and when the sun was up, they were scorched, and because they had no root, they withered away. And some fell among thorns: and the thorns sprung up and choked them. But other fell into good ground, and brought forth fruit, some a hundredfold, some sixtyfold, some thirtyfold,*" all modern readers understand that the story is not about a ploughman and about his experiences, but the ploughman just symbolises something as we read a parable. It is about religious teaching. The chance of yielding good fruit does not only depend on the teaching, but also depends on the soil in which it is sowed—meaning that the soul of a believer is necessary in order for these teachings to take root and generate good deeds, or, just the contrary, the seed of the teaching can be quickly accepted but later, whenever a temptation occurs, the fruits of the teaching get dried. It can also occur that Evil conceals the seed and can stop it from producing fruits. The modern readers can also understand this sort of parable but they do not know that the writers of these parables could also make events appear as if they actually happened, though they only wanted to use a parable, in order to represent the truth, which this parable symbolises. For this reason, they cannot understand the true nature of the Gospels. That is why we cannot reject the narrative on the basis it's not listing true facts. These stories should be read as poetic parables and in this way we can discover the deepest truth, which they do express. Goethe was right in saying this:

> Der menschliche Geist kann sich strecken wie er will: jene Klarheit und Reinheit der Ethik, wie sie in den menschlichen schimmert und leuchtet, wird er nicht übersteigen.

[Artur cites Goethe in German. I (Artur's granddaughter, Zsuzsi Renyi) will try to give an English translation with the help of a colleague, who studied German literature, but it is not the authentic translation as the original book, where the quotation was chosen from, could not be traced. So in English: "The human spirit can never surpass the clarity and purity of Ethics as it humanly shimmers and shines."]

One of my tasks was to introduce the Gospels' stories as deep, poetic parables. I am going to point out those psychological contexts, which the human spirit could just discover following the 2,000 years of the development of modern psychology. While psychology can only include these truths, the Gospels 2,000 years ago did completely express these truths better than psychology or even psychoanalysis does in our day.

I do not want to go into details now but would like to refer to another aspect as well. This aspect can only be understood in case we interpret the stories of the Gospels—I mean, the laws and commands of the Gospels—as poetic parables.

Our contemporary views are also wrong in this respect. They regard the laws and commands of the Gospels as military commands or state laws, which must be strictly kept. They regard those commands of the Gospels as present day instructions or orders, the breaching of which would lead to imprisonment. We can only point out that the commands of the Gospels cannot be followed literally, just the contrary; the literal interpretation of these commands would be wrong. For example, that command of the Gospels, "Whosoever shall smite thee on thy right cheek, turn to him the other also." If anyone would interpret this command literally and would not defend himself when attacked in a dark street at night by a robber or a murderer, that person completely misunderstands the Gospels' commands, or he does not understand them in the right way. At the same time one should not reject these commands just because they are thought to be wrong or because one thinks these commands cannot be fulfilled. The commands of the Gospels are poetic exaggerations (just as poetic imagery is also based on exaggerations). These poetic exaggerations involve valuable advice as well: namely, it means a nobler mentality enduring an attack or letting it go on than defending ourselves and fighting back immediately, because this noble passivity can express our superiority better than the behaviour of an attacker.

The same is true regarding all the commands and laws of the Gospels. Following these instructions literally is completely impossible, but their message is deeply true and good, if only we can regard them as poetic exaggerations.

I would like to refer to a third aspect as well, the misunderstandings of translations. A lot of mistakes were made when translating the original text. All the more so as the language changes continuously. That is why the people of our age misunderstand the translations that were done long ago. I refer to an example which occurred in the translation of the text of *The Sermon on the Mount*. The translator might have thought he provided a comprehensible translation, which was adequate for his own time: "Blessed are the poor in spirit for theirs is the kingdom of heaven."

In the contemporary Hungarian language, the phrase for *poor in spirit* refers to a person who does not have a spiritual richness, or is primitive or stupid or uneducated. It is impossible that just Jesus would praise these sort of people. He encouraged people in his *Sermon on the Mount*, "*Lay not up for yourselves treasures upon earth.*" The explanation lies in the misunderstandings of translations. Poor in spirit does not refer to a person who is poor in his feelings but on the contrary, it refers to people who are similar in spirit to those who are poor in an economic sense. These poor people can understand the sorrows of their fellow sufferers based on their own experiences and, therefore, these people are understanding and merciful. Mercifulness is rare among rich people; just the opposite was true: in the age of the Gospels' narrative this understanding nature of poor people was an accepted truth. Mercifulness was called *misericordia* in Latin, following the denomination referring to poor people, who were called *miser* or *misericors* in Latin, meaning their hearts are similar to those of poor people, so they are merciful. Therefore, this is the way we should read and interpret the Gospels, we should avoid misunderstandings and mistranslations, and we should regard the narrative of the Gospels as parables. We should interpret their commands as poetic exaggerations. If we do so, we will understand that this writing is of the highest value of the human spirit, which can set an example for humanity for thousands of years.

I also wrote my interpretation of *The Sermon on the Mount* in English. Most of the typing was Mommy's work. I admired the way she learned how to type and spell in English. I still have the handwritten copy of this study of mine as it has not been published. Gisele Johnson, a Norwegian bishop—with whom we made friends later—liked my study very much and advised me to send a copy to one of his friends in England. This friend was an Anglican vicar of Jewish origin. The vicar also liked my paper and he only criticised some insignificant parts, yet he could not support its publication, saying he was too busy to do it. I wrote to many English publishers, but received only negative answers. Then I stopped seeking a publisher and thought, sooner or later, the right time for its publication would arrive.

We spent the summer of 1921 in the Bimbo Street house of my mother. It was a detached house with a terrace looking out to the street and a veranda overlooking the big, shady garden. One could feel as if it was in a small village but actually it was only some miles from the centre of Budapest. My late father bought the house with the garden in 1894, rebuilt the house, and he often gardened there. The garden was his small empire. My mother later had to sell off some parcels of the big garden, but still we had a lawn with flower beds and had lots of lilacs and jasmine bushes. It was an ideal place for children to play.

This year the liquidation of our company was almost complete and I could deal with other matters. For example, the wife of my former classmate had a garden with a horticultural greenhouse on Trombitas Street, in the Buda part of Budapest, and I was asked to do some consulting work there as an engineer. I planned the greenhouse's heating system and I had to buy, among other things, a boiler, the pipe system, window frames, window glasses, bricks, and so on. At the end of this year I undertook a bigger consulting job and enlarged the trunk factory located on my brother's site in Pestlorinc, a suburb of Pest. We also attached a manufacturing factory to that. This job was finished in the spring of 1922 but later I was also asked to do some work in connection with that factory and then I received a regular income. I did complete an engineering job in the so-called Flora Factory that belonged to my brother's family.

At the end of 1920 Grandpa and Grandma left Switzerland for Badenweiler. Regina Alexander, your Grandma, survived another brain stroke and this time she was unable to leave her bed. They spent all of 1921 there and in February of 1922 Mummy travelled to Badenweiler for three weeks to see her mother again. She took a picture of Buba with her to show Regina, who said, "*Süss*", sweet in German, after she saw it.

We spent the summer of 1922 again in the Bimbo Street house, and in the autumn of 1922 Mommy's mother died in Badenweiler. Mommy travelled there for her burial ceremony and returned home in deep grief. [Regina Broessler was buried in Germany though there is a headstone in the Kozma Street Jewish Cemetery in Budapest with her name on it; her husband is buried in this grave.]

The same year, between the end of May and the third week of June, I visited my emigrant friend, Adolph, in Castel Gandolfo, Italy. Fascism has already taken hold in Italy, but in these early days it was relatively harmless. The traveller, who came from a far country, or emigrants like Adolph, did not experience much of it. I was much more touched by the cheerful vitality of the Italian people that differed favourably from the doom and gloom I saw in rural Hungarian life. I recalled Ady's words [Ady Endre, 1877–1919, famous poet] that here we are a sad nation dwelling on the two banks of the Danube, which is still unable to be happy, while in Italy, happiness can be felt during big celebrations, processions, and during religious feasts. I think that was the reason that the first few years of fascism were so relatively harmless; we could not even anticipate the horrors that it became, first in Germany, and then elsewhere, when fascism changed a nation of singing people to a nation of sergeants.

In this summer of 1922, when we stayed in Bimbo Street in my mother's house, Buba could already speak. We recorded his words in an album that also contained stories of little Buba. Once, when Mommy and he were staying in the garden, and Mommy then still had long hair (later on it was cut shorter), and Mommy's head covered Buba's face, Buba said this: Mommy's long hair mantels Buba's little head like, he paused for a while, like a cloud covers the sun.

Dadi [meaning Nanny], whom I met in Ebenhausen where she took care of Judith, Magda's daughter, came to work for us in 1921 or in 1922. She and Buba grew to love each other very much and she taught him the Transdanubian Hungarian dialect and told him many stories about the little Jesus. [In Hungarian folk culture the baby Jesus was called little Jesus.]

During Christmas of 1922, when Buba was one year and nine months old and he was allowed to come into our living room to see the glittering Christmas tree, he went to the tree and bowed to it and said with affection: *Thanks so much, my little Jesus*. [In folk stories little Jesus brings Christmas presents for children.]

You, my Buba, loved this living room, which was full of books in the bookshelves up to the ceiling and your favourite books were the encyclopaedias, full of coloured pictures. But

Mommy was concerned for these books and tried to keep them safe. If you had happened to tear one of the pages (which actually you never did) Grandpa would have been very upset. That was why you were asked not to touch these encyclopaedia. The next story regarding these books and also recorded in your book was this: the university sent us a photo of Grandpa, sitting at a table, together with some deans of the same university, all of them looking so grouchy, one might think that the photographer put their heads into a frame, as it was a custom at that time. You saw their stern looks and interpreted it that the Daddies are upset and are telling me not to touch the big books.

In 1923 Grandpa moved from Badenweiler to Kiel, then to Nowawes, next to Berlin and Potsdam, and I also travelled there to see him and discuss the details of his moving. Grandma Alexander's former faithful nurse followed him there to run his household. At the beginning of March or maybe in February, I travelled there to talk to Grandpa (and to fix the details for his return home). These were quite busy times in our family: Erzsi left her husband, Miklos Gyorgy, and went to Paris and later sailed to America with Sicu Major [Henry Major], who was twelve years younger. Lili was also there with us in Berlin. Feri [Dr Franz Alexander] also lived in Berlin at that time but I only saw him once.

An interesting thing happened to Grandpa when he travelled to Berlin to buy a new Dunhill pipe with all its accessories and some tobacco in a Wertheim shop. It was all wrapped in a neat package that he put next to him on a seat on the train back to Nowawes. When he stood up to get off he was surprised to see such a fine, big package on the next seat, and thought that someone had left it behind. He went to the stationmaster's office and deposited it, supposing the person who left it on the train would return for it. The stationmaster took his name and information and asked if he wanted a reward. He said he did not and went home. At home his old housekeeper asked him, "Nun, Herr Professor, und die Pfeife?" [meaning: "Well,

Professor Alexander, what about the pipes?"]. It was not until then that he realised what had happened and replied, "An der Station angegeben, als gefunden" [meaning: "I left it at the station at the lost and found"]. He returned to the railway station and told the stationmaster that the package belonged to him. "Well, you yourself deposited that parcel as lost property," said the surprised stationmaster. "Yes, I've just forgotten it was mine." They all laughed and as he could describe the contents of the package in detail he could finally receive it. I think that was a classic case of the absent-mindedness of professors, which we often recalled laughingly.

During my travel I experienced the Weimar Germany which did not impress me favourably. In the background there were Hitler's terrible acts but we still considered that world to be far away and we did not take it too seriously. There was extreme inflation in Germany and I think it was a deliberate policy of the German National Socialist Party to annualise the foreign financial claims (in marks). On the other hand, generating inflation was favourable for big business to make profits. This manoeuvre was carried out with the typical German efficiency and, as a consequence, it resulted in quite dreary circumstances.

One could see banknotes everywhere in the streets, all over the pavements. You could tell how serious the inflation was when larger and larger banknotes were tossed away into the streets. There were 100, 500, and sometimes 1,000 mark banknotes all over the pavements. The 1,000 mark banknote was only worth a penny at that time. For example, when I bought a *Berliner Tageblatt*, a Berlin daily newspaper, at a news-stand, I saw a pile of 1,000 mark banknotes in a box. The price of a daily paper was twenty times a 1,000 mark banknote and later even that price increased. The banknotes were printed on beautiful sheets of paper woven with linen. As there were few 10,000 mark banknotes, people mostly used the 1,000 mark banknotes for cash transactions. I asked the newsagent if he took these notes to a bank at the end of his workday in order to exchange them for bigger denominations. He told me he took them into a paper mill, as he could be paid 200,000 marks more for one thousand pieces of 1,000 mark banknotes. I believed it as this big-sized, outstanding quality paper money was worth more to the paper mill. At the same time security was poor as well as the illumination and the hygienic state of the streets—however, all these were not as awful as what was to follow later.

I knew only one person in Berlin, Professor Paul Horing. He was teaching at the Charlottenburg Technical University of Berlin. Professor Paul Horing was both a nice and good person and had a wide range of intellectual interests. He travelled all over the world and—I think—he could not be considered a typical German person. Actually he came from Württemberg. It is just that corner of Germany that was the fatherland of such people as the Hauffs, the Schillers, and the Uhlands—all of whom distanced themselves from the Prussian mentality. [Artur refers to a sort of rigid punctuality and non-flexible mentality by using the phrase Prussian mentality: that is the way we do refer to that in Hungary.]

I was not able to meet with Professor Paul Horing because he had died the year earlier. I planned to visit his widow and nine children but finally ran out of time. I returned to Pest and at the end of March 1923, Granddad also arrived back home. He was quite pleased to be home and Mommy was especially happy to welcome him in his home that she had furnished for him so carefully. You, Buba were also very happy with his return. Two pictures of him were hanging on the wall, a new one, and another one that showed him as a twenty-two- or twenty-three-year-old young man in Paris. When Granddad arrived home, you pointed at his latest picture and said: *This Grandpa has already arrived home*. Then you pointed to the other picture: *This Grandpa has not arrived yet*.

That is how our life together with Granddad began, a life that lasted until his death in October 1927. These were very happy times for us. In the beginning, I have to admit, it was difficult for me as a young husband when Mommy always favoured her daddy instead of me. Mommy told me later that it was also painful for her but she felt this was her duty and she was actually right. However, I believe I proved myself and passed the test. I had an almost perfect father-son relationship with Granddad. I heard from other people that he was talking about me in such a favourable way which I do not even dare write down. He really appreciated me unjustifiably. We never had a true conflict though on one slight occasion he was angry with me as I defended someone to whom I believed he spoke too harshly. He was angry only for twelve minutes during a lunchtime. However, when I saw how badly he felt about the fact that I did not fully accept his opinion, I went into his room after lunch and explained to him that this was not against him. When he saw how important it was for me not to hurt him, tears came to his eyes and he hugged me and offered his hand to me and so again we were in complete peace with each other.

I tried to be as useful for him as possible, I carried on a correspondence with English publishing houses to publish his works on Shakespeare, and also translated some chapters into English. I also showed him my writings and asked for his opinion, and he also helped me with recommendations to editors and publishers, such as Mr Ranschburg, the manager of Pantheon Publishing, who commissioned me later with the translation of three novels of H. G. Wells. He also introduced me to Mr Jeno Heltai [1871–1957, writer] who was the head of Athenaeum Publishing at that time and who commissioned me to translate one of Bourget's novels. He wanted me to be a member of the Pen Club, which was being formed, but finally it could not be established. It was also Granddad who recommended me to my employer, the Ganz Factory where I became an employee and worked for decades. [Ganz Electric Works and Rail Factory was founded in Buda by Abraham Ganz in 1885.]

He only said some critical words about me late in the summer of 1927 and, as far as I can remember, it was some insignificant matter; however, this misunderstanding may be the reason why the relationship between me and Mommy's sisters and brothers is not as good as I would have liked it to be. I still hope that our relationship will improve as time goes by. Erzsi, for example, now writes more kindly than she did in her first letter.

These years were the happiest ones for Mommy as she was able to look after us, she could use her goodness and be a good wife, a good daughter, and a good mother all at the same time. At Granddad's seventy-fifth birthday Tamas Kobor [1867–1942, writer] said, "He returned home to his Borka." Tamas Kobor also spoke about Mommy's happiness and about how delighted she was to be able take care of Daddy. She created a paradise for her father in her home where he could invite his friends, who were faithful to him, and who respected and loved him. Kobor also mentioned how happy Alexander appeared to be in his home, where Mommy created a lovely and peaceful space for him to enjoy in his old age, as much as was possible. She also created happiness for me and it should not be taken too seriously that I was put in the position of second fiddle to her daddy.

There were a few occasions when both Granddad and I wanted to invite our friends and his wishes were given priority. But I treated these matters as insignificant and tried to help Mommy provide everything that was pleasant for her father. At the same time, Mommy was also a unique mother for you, my Buba; one that was unmatched in the world. I do believe and do hope that she herself was also happy. As, in my view, one who is as good as she was, could be nothing but happy.

Mommy travelled to Italy with her father for the first time in 1923. They left in May and stayed in Rimini for four weeks. Unfortunately, Granddad fell ill in Rimini. They then stayed in Florence for another week, where Granddad recovered, and finally they voyaged home. Originally they also wanted to visit Rome, but they could not manage to travel there during the visit.

We spent that summer again in my mother's home on Bimbo Street where Granddad also joined us. It was there that we received the sad news that my sister's, Bela Auer, first husband had died.

As far as I can remember, my second journey to Italy took place in the autumn of the same year, 1923, when I went to see my old friend, Adolf. He was able to find a good job working for his friend, Dr Leander Tomarkin, who was the inventor of a sort of medicine, called *antimirobum Tomarkin*, which was a forerunner of the sulphur drugs which are used nowadays. He was the trade manager of a laboratory where these medicines were manufactured. I also met Tomarkin, a nice, amusing, and talented person whose medicine was something brand new and significant. On the other hand, he also had some features of a *swindler*, con man, and a madman. (*NB. He was not a physician and was, in fact, an imposter. He did not go to medical school, dropped out of university with poor grades, and spent time experimenting in his father's laboratory. He had gained a reputation after "treating" Victor Emmanuel in Rome.*) This medicine could be used primarily to cure pneumonia and at the time Pope Benedict XV fell ill with pneumonia. Tomarkin went to see the eighty-year-old Professor Ettore Marchiafava, who was the medical doctor at the Vatican. Tomarkin suggested that he could cure the pope. Professor Marchiafava asked Tomarkin what sort of tests were done to assure his cure would work. He answered he could only test mice. "I am sorry," answered Professor Marchiafava. "I trust in your medicine but you can understand that the pope cannot be an experimental guinea pig for a medicine which has not been tested on humans yet." Tomarkin answered: "I am sorry but in this case the pope is going to die," and he actually died soon after. Tomarkin was called by Professor Marchiafava a few months later and was told that he would provide him a laboratory to test his medicine. The professor also provided him a ward in Santo Spirito Hospital with forty patients, all of them suffering with pneumonia. There was also a control group of another forty patients, all of them suffering from pneumonia, who would be treated by the old method. The results substantiated Tomarkin's method perfectly, in that twenty per cent of the patients who were suffering from pneumonia and were treated by the old method died, while all of Tomarkin's patients recovered. The queen herself paid attention to this result and furnished a laboratory for Dr Tomarkin in Quirinal.

This time I could discover more of Rome than on previous trips. I also went to see a museum, next to the railway station. On the stairs of the museum a lady asked me in Italian: "Are you the manager of the museum?"' I answered her in Hungarian: "No, I am not but if I am right you are Noemi Kobor."' That was right, she stayed in Rome with Mrs Agai. I was also invited by them to stay and I introduced them to Adolf and Dr Tomarkin. Tomarkin fell in love with her, proposed to her, and Noemi gave him a positive answer. But some weeks later, when Noemi returned to Rome with her father, Tomarkin changed his mind and the marriage never took place. Tamas Kobor was also accompanied by Mommy and Granddad, they stayed some weeks there. Granddad threw a ten centime coin into the Trevi fountain, but unfortunately it was his last visit to Rome, and the myth of throwing a coin in the fountain to assure a future visit did not work. I think I am wrong, it was not the end of 1923 but instead the spring of 1924 when Noemi and her father returned to Rome.

In the spring of 1923 Mommy continued with her photography in a workshop on Jozsef Street. Her main interest was special photography techniques and, together with a colleague of hers who was a painter, she took photos that were coloured by painting. She also made some copperplates using a new technique. Most of my work at that time was English translations for technical patent agents as well as some literary translations.

Apart from the three novels of H. G. Wells, and that of Bourget, I also translated a novel of Philips, which was praised by critics. A second edition of one of the Wells novels was also ordered because the first edition sold out quickly.

I have to tell an anecdote about Mommy which categorised her very well and I often pulled her leg because of it. She took care of the characters in a novel as if they were actual living persons. Once, when the hero was busy and had adventures both before and after noon, she told me: "Oh, poor one, he has not had lunch yet!" I laughed a lot, though this remark characterised her well and showed her childish nature which regarded a tale as reality. On the other hand I think it also mirrored her goodness, helpfulness, and caring nature which also involved caring about the lunch of a make-believe character. She typed my translations and did so with special care and commitment. In spite of not having a perfect command of English, she could type these texts without mistakes. Even this small detail shows a lot of love, care, and conscientiousness.

We also spent the summer of 1924 in Bimbo Street at my mother's place, while my mother was treated in a sanatorium in Dresden, Germany, run by Dr Lahmann. This took place when Germany was suffering a raging inflation.

CHAPTER THREE

Work and politics

Meanwhile in Hungary the counter-revolution gradually ended and the era of the so-called "Bethlen-consolidation" began. [Estvan Bethlen's government was in power from 1921–1931 and aimed to achieve political consolidation.] The political pressure exerted earlier on Granddad eased and he returned to his work as a journalist at *Pester Lloyd*. He wrote perfect articles on the topic of aesthetics week after week and he also began working on an essay about John Stuart Mill. His book on Spinoza had already been published by that time.

We led a very active social life and many of Granddad's friends came to see him frequently. I recollect my good friend, poor Frigyes Karinthy [famous Hungarian writer and humourist; "poor" refers to his brain tumour, which caused an early death] came to visit during those times. I remember some evenings, when we played a game, invented by Karinthy, which was fun and all because of his outstanding cleverness.

Once, when Tamas Kobor came to one of our parties, I introduced my graphology analysis as a kind of party game. I remember I was successful at a party, in Margit Veszi's home, during the autumn of 1918, when I did that kind of handwriting analysis for the guests: "This person is an Austrian naval officer, who can only speak broken Hungarian, but in spite of want him to "love" Jews, but we wanted someone who does not feel any distinction between Jews and non-Jews in neither a positive nor a negative way. It also turned out that he did not find our family "Jewish enough". He preferred religious, traditional Jews, who kept rites and even orthodox Jews; however, he liked us personally to the extent that he forgave us that we were not religious people.

It took me another twenty years to find out what he really wanted of Jewish people. Apart from his free-thinking attitude and his brave criticism of the Church, he accepted the teachings of his Church that considers Jesus a Saviour, saying he is Christ, the Messiah. (The word "Christos" is the Greek translation of the Hebrew word for "Messiah".) Therefore, according to them in the person of Jesus the Messiah arrived, who was foretold by the prophet Isaiah. Gisle Johnson thought that the Christian Church was hurt by the Jews because the latter were the repositories of the teachings of the Old Testament and that of the prophet Isaiah. Therefore, the Jews do not accept that the Messiah has already arrived, but they are still looking forward to his arrival. Johnson wanted to find such an orthodox Jew, who could deeply believe that everything that was predicted by the prophet Isaiah should definitely come true. This person should accept that Jesus was the Messiah.

Johnson's effort was basically absurd. He could have found even 1,000 orthodox Jewish people among the "religious " Jews, who believe nowadays as if everything that was predicted by the prophet Isaiah 2,400 years ago should be literally true. On the other hand, it cannot be expected that such a man, who is so strongly stuck to the Jewish tradition, should be exempt from the same constraint, that he should liberate himself of the other, also 2,000-year-old Jewish tradition, according to which Jesus was not the Messiah. This assumption should suggest such an extent of the sticking to the traditions and at the same time liberation of the same traditions in the mind of the same person, which is naturally impossible. Johnson was not satisfied if someone—like myself—discovered the highest level of human wisdom and goodness in Jesus's teachings: he wanted a rigid insisting on the belief that one should identify Jesus with the Messiah, as it was predicted by the prophet Isaiah. That was why our spiritual co-operation could not develop further, though he sent my study on *The Sermon on the Mount* to one of his British friends.

It seemed that his wife supported him in every respect yet she could not accept this friendship with Jewish people. This could provide an explanation for her mysterious behaviour towards us. After visiting each other for a decade and following Johnson's fantastic lecture about Norway, during one of our Wednesday evening debate circles his wife suddenly "forgot" about our invitation for dinner. Later, when we repeatedly invited them she rejected our invitations and sent us a telegram, referring to "some unexpected hindrance" and did not call us to explain, though calling us would have been much simpler. She completely stopped meeting us. I did not understand the situation. After some years passed I asked Mommy to call them in spite of the above-mentioned incident. Mommy called her and the wife of the priest told her the following: "You are an angel, please, forgive me." Then our friendly contact began again. I will tell you now how our friendship changed during that period of persecution.

Returning to my graphology journalism: my work as a journalist began in November 1924 and ended in May 1925 when I stopping writing the graphology column. My reason to do so was that I was fed up with graphology and felt that this sort of business, i.e., analysing in bulk inevitably leads to poor quality. Most people's writings are not interesting at all and do not tell anything about their author—however, in this position something had to be said in order to do one's job. Since then I did not undertake any more graphology tasks with a few exceptions, because I did not want to become a graphologist and wanted to forget this episode in my life.

However, this activity had its advantages, meeting interesting people like the Johnsons and Klager, who is the only handwriting analyst doing this activity scientifically. He also wrote some books on the topic based on the general philosophy of characterology. I met a very interesting person in getting to know him. I regard him as an interesting philosopher and his writings influenced me a lot. I especially appreciated many of his critical remarks about psychoanalysis. I was well paid for the graphology work and I could support the maintenance of our home and provide for all of us.

I worked a lot in those days. I translated fiction, I did translations of patents and science-popularising articles, and analysed lots of graphology writings (actually 1,500 pieces of handwriting over six or seven months) and wrote long pages of analyses. Mommy typed them all; I was hardly able to do all of these.

I worked many nights until sunrise the next day. I could only tolerate it for the sake of Mommy and for you, my Buba. And for the two of you I did not only tolerate working a lot, but I was even happy to be able to do all that.

However, I reached a decision that wasn't as easy as simply working a lot. I decided that in spite of freelancing jobs and the good income from them, if I had a permanent job that would ease Mommy's worries about our budget. We could then expect a fixed sum on the first day of every month irrespective of the changes in the prosperity of the workforce market.

That was a difficult decision to make. Though I worked regularly, I insisted on a free timetable for myself. Therefore, this responsibility, namely being present at a firm every single day "ob schön ob regen" [he wrote this in German, meaning "come rain or shine"], furthermore quite early in the morning, was something very unsuited to me.

Nevertheless, I took the job and kept it for almost twenty years for Mommy and for you, my Buba. At the beginning I had to be satisfied with quite a low salary. As a beginner

I received a salary of only four million koronas [contemporary Hungarian currency], which was equivalent to 320 pengos [another Hungarian currency of that period]. I was aware that it would increase and actually, in some months' time, it rose to 800 pengos, later reached 1,000 pengos and remained at this level between 1928 and 1944 with small fluctuations. My salary was somewhat less for a year or two at the time of the great world depression of 1931. Later on I received extra payment for working overtime for Mr Klein and, therefore, my salary was actually somewhat higher. Besides working for the Ganz factory, I still had time to do extra work, namely translations, for which I earned 6,000 to 7,000 pengos annually and once only 4,000 pengos. In 1938 I received much more interpretation jobs in connection with the wave of emigration, which paid 16,000 to 20,000 pengos.

On average I could count on 12,000 pengos salary, paid by Ganz factory between 1928 and 1944, plus another 8,000 pengos income, paid by the extra commissions, therefore I earned altogether 20,000 pengos annually. Mommy's income by taking photographs added to that. In most years she earned only 3,000 to 4,000 pengos but there were years when this sum was over 10,000 pengos. As we did not have any expensive hobbies we could manage to provide a cosy and easy but not a luxurious life. We always had everything we needed: we could afford to have a summer holiday and other vacations. We only had economic difficulties during the years of the world depression, when we had small debts. Sometimes we asked for an advance payment on my salary, but we could always repay these loans and eventually we could balance our budget.

We also had to pay some extra costs, such as the eleven months-long visit of Pali and his family, meaning Pali, Covi, and Kato [first daughter Catherine] plus their maid, but we could also manage that as I had inherited a part of the house in Buda after the death of my mother. Later we sold that part of the house for 30,000 pengos. We did not feel sorry to make the sacrifice, we only felt sorry for their reaction which was just the opposite of what we hoped for. But we forgave them that as well.

Well, I began working for the Ganz works on 25 June 1925. However, we immediately went on holiday, spending more than a month in Italy. I actually began work on the 1st of August. We spent that July in Grado (near Gorizia). I know you can also recall it, my Buba. At that time you were four years and four months old. You can certainly remember the beach, the husband of Klari Rovo, whom you called "uncle Chocolate" and you may remember Boriska Szirmai, and another lady whom you called Aunt Szemere and to whom you told the following at the playground: "You are not the mother of Tommy, because Uncle Szemere is both his mother and father at the same time." You can certainly recall the memory of the brown teddy bear, which was lost while we were travelling and I was desperate to find it. You can remember our flat, next to the lagoon, and the little girl, for whom "little periwinkle should be shown". Maybe you can also recollect the rhymes, which you told, addressed to the sea. Do you also remember our outing to the island of shells, where you lost your sandals? However, you probably mix it up with our second summer in Grado in 1926. It was this second summer that Vera also arrived to see us—you called her "Little V" [Vera is Paul and Covi Alexander's second daughter].

So I began working for the Ganz factory on the 1st of August and that brought some regularity to our life. I left at 7.30 am every day, first to get a shave at the barber's on Iranyi Street, and then I took tram number 26 to the Ganz works in order to arrive there at exactly 8.10 am. Many years passed until I was allowed to arrive later, at 9.30 am, in exchange for doing so much overtime into the late evening hours. At that time there was no canteen in the factory, so Mommy packed me sandwiches for brunch. At 3 pm my official working day ended and I went home. I had dinner and afterwards I began my translation work at home. I usually dictated it to Mommy, who typed until only 7 pm. In the evening we had supper, enjoyed good conversations with Granddad, sometimes we invited guests, sometimes we went out to a cinema. We had two housekeepers, Margit and Juliska, they were sisters, and we also had Dadi [meaning "Nanny"]. You, my Buba developed perfectly. We noted your cutest sayings, such as: "There are three things hanging in my stomach: goodness, badness, and angriness. If badness tumbles, I am bad, if angriness tumbles, I am angry."

Then we asked you, "And what about goodness?" "Goodness always works," you replied. Granddad felt this was especially worth remembering and told Mommy to ask Buba about that again the next day and said if he answered the same that would mean this was his original idea. Therefore Mommy did this and you gave the same answer.

So Christmas arrived that year as it did every year. Mommy arranged everything perfectly and in the most beautiful way. She gave some surprise presents to everybody: for Granddad, for you, my Buba, and for me. I also bought her something, which she liked, and I expected her to be happy with that and actually she was very happy because she could appreciate even odds and ends.

I suppose it was that year, in 1925, that Judit, Magda's daughter, spent Christmas with us and she played the role of the angel, and you, my Buba, considered her to be an angel and, even later, you actually refused to acknowledge that she was not an angel. Our friends also brought presents for you: Tamas Kobor gave you a fantastic electric locomotive which ran on tracks. My old friend, Doctor Lajos Goldenberg gave you an electric tram. We had a beautiful, high Christmas tree that reached the ceiling and there were sparklers and chocolate and candies on it. And above all there was Mommy, and Mommy was happiness herself.

I am sure she must have been happy herself as well, she, who was able to generate so much happiness. She must have been happy, in spite of her tragically short lifetime and I must find comfort in this thought.

I have already been writing about the year 1930, when I spent a part of the summer in Nevi, Italy with Adolf and his family. But I missed Borka very much and therefore I travelled to Lunz am Seeben where she was staying with Lili Hajdu. [She was Mrs Miklos Gimes, 1891–1960, Borka's very close friend, an influential psychiatrist and psychoanalyst. Her husband died in a concentration camp and her son, also called Miklos Gimes, was killed by retortion for the 1956 revolution together with Imre Nagy, the martyred prime minister, in the very same "legal" action.] We spent a lovely twelve days there. Agnes Rozgonyi was always in a good mood which gave off a glow to all of us. Besides being an outstanding violinist, she could tell lots of jokes. Her friend Lili Balazs often came to see us and sometimes we organised bridge parties. Mommy, Lili Hajdu, Lili Balazs, and Mignon were the players. [Mignon is a nickname.] This group sprang from previous bridge party get-togethers held in a Buda kiosk cafe. I cannot remember anything special from the second part of this year. I tried to obtain my appointment as an interpreter, but there were some difficulties due to a certain official's interference. However, finally I managed to get my appointment with help from one of my former classmates, Tibor Zsitvay, who was a minister at that time. Paul Nyari helped me remember this fact. So I asked for an appointment with the minister, who recognised me immediately, and who would appoint me in a week. On the 15th of December in 1930 I managed to pass the interpreters examination.

So we reached the year 1931. This was the first year when the optimism of the post-war years, with the expectations of eternal/lasting peace and the establishment of a new world, were altered by a bad social atmosphere. We had doubts characterised as we sensed the coming terrible events that took the form of a worldwide economic depression. The depression began in the spring of 1931, with the bankruptcy of the Vienna

Creditanstalt, and this generated an overall period of austerity and the ghost of unemployment appeared everywhere.

I was not worried about being fired from the Ganz factory: I had become too indispensable. I had been appointed as a main supervisor when the Ganz factory built a power line and electric works in Banhida in collaboration with the English Electric Company. It was a big job which cost 35 million pengos and provided approximately fifty per cent of the electric supply of Budapest, even today [remember, Artur is writing this in 1947]. The British and Hungarian engineering teams could not understand each other's languages. The Bible gives an extremely precise description of how the Tower of Babel collapsed because of the problem of the builders not understanding each other. This could conceivably happen in the case of these engineers, who do not understand each other yet want to build and work together. For example, the team that builds the ground floor of a building sends a message to the team that builds the first floor that the ceiling of the ground floor can be loaded by a weight of 100 pounds per square inch and the other team misunderstands that and means 100 kilograms (that is fourteen times the intended weight), then this floor would certainly collapse. My task was to avoid such a situation with my translation.

In three and a half years I translated 7,000 papers into English, or from English into Hungarian. The length of these translations ranged from a few lines to 300 page-long texts. The text of the offer at the beginning of the working collaboration was 300 pages long. Mr Klein, the top vice manager, made me translate that text in a week, keeping me in the factory every evening until 11 pm and, on the last night, I worked all night, into the early hours of the morning. I dictated to personnel sitting at typewriters, who were being changed constantly, and everything was finished and ready by the next morning so that Mr Klein could then bring the translated texts to the ministry. I received a special bonus of 500 pengos from Mr Klein and the typewriters/stenographers were also given 100–200 pengos each.

Nobody could duplicate my accomplishment and that was why I did not worry about being fired, in spite of the panic generated by the layoff or fire notices. However, Mr Klein used this panic in order to create a "terror mill", and nobody could be free from that, I could not either. The following seven or eight years, until Mr Klein left for South America in 1938 or 1939, were filled with gradually increasing overtime work at the factory and by our attempts to defend ourselves against the practice. There was hardly any time to do anything else. It was terrible how the 700 workers and the 700 office workers suffered from their fear of this mentally ill person.

Later on I managed to get the pleasure and permission to come to work by half past nine because of the evenings spent in training. When I arrived one day, I found some letters in English in the ominous grey envelopes with a note saying, "Mr Klein, the manager insists on discussing the matter today." I had to go and see Mr Klein's secretary and waited for hours in his anteroom; I was not allowed to leave that room even for a minute. Finally my turn arrived and Mr Klein dictated his answers to me in Hungarian. I returned to my room, dictated the letters in English, and returned to wait for his signature. Our shift was over at 3 pm but obviously I could not go home yet.

Sometimes I received a telephone message at 6 pm, instructing me to bring the letters to the tram factory in Buda in order for them to be signed. I travelled there on the tram and waited, again. As I waited, I felt as though I were on the porch of Hell. Finally Mr Klein signed the letters at 8.30 pm. He often criticised a word or a phrase and if that happened, I travelled back to Kobanyai Road, where poor typist girls were waiting, and I had to make the corrections. It was regarded a special favour if the attendant took the corrected letters to Mr Klein's villa on Rozsadomb. If he was cross with me, as when I protested about overtime the previous day, it was I who had to go to the villa as well. He called it "applying a sanction" and on these occasions

I arrived by midnight. There were occasions when I only got home at 2.30 am after such Klein-type overtime episodes.

I tolerated all sorts of torture with an exceptional grace. That was also Mommy's quality, not mine, but I did everything for her with pleasure.

Besides doing all that I had to do my private work as well. I had many private translations and received 5,000 to 8,000 pengos a year for that work. (In 1938, because of the wave of emigration leading to additional work, I earned 15,000 to 16,000 pengos but that was an exceptional year.)

I called these events "evening news" using the Hungarian sense of the word that also sounds like "news" but means torture. These evening news sessions of Mr Klein's did not occur every day. I can't imagine now how I could have tolerated it. I worked an average of eleven hours a day and sometimes I had to work thirteen or sixteen hours. Mommy always assisted me to make sure all my private work was done. When I did interpretations, she did a lot of work by herself because I prepared translation samples for her to use as a guide.

We finished working on Banhida in 1932 but there were new projects. One new project was the electrification (the Ganz factory co-operated with Metropolitan Vickers then) and another the motorised railway carriages, transported to South America, in co-operation with General Electric Co. The offers or proposals often had to be translated into English but also into Spanish. (Over many years 222 railway carriages were transported to South America and this generated lots of translating work.)

I can recollect that Buba stayed in Runau in the year 1931, at a summer camp organised by individual psychologists, with a group of other children. Borka went to see him and afterwards met Erzsi in Austria (I think in Gmunken), where Erzsi stayed with some American student actresses.

Payments to the Ganz factory decreased as a consequence of the worldwide depression in 1931. When I had to work overtime I obviously had less time to do my private work.

These years were, then, more difficult from a financial point of view. We often had to apply for small loans or request an advance on my salary. We could completely improve our financial situation only in 1938 with this additional private income.

I cannot remember all of our holidays during these years; Buba might be able to fill in the missing information. We often stayed at Lepence [a resort on the banks of the Danube, not far from Budapest] but I do not know which year these vacations took place. As far as I remember, we went to Veroce in 1932 with Pali's family and in that year Feri and the Rosenwald family came to see us there. In 1933 we stayed at God [near Veroce], also with Pali's family, and the following year we also stayed at God, again with Pali's family. Feri came to see us for a second time that year and Pali and his family immigrated to Belgium soon thereafter. In 1935 we stayed in Veroce and also in the early part of the summer of 1935 Borka travelled to the Netherlands. But I have to rethink the chronology of these events more carefully. I must stress the fact that we always went on holiday with Pali and his family, all of whom Borka loved greatly. I cannot remember anybody, anywhere who expressed such a love as Borka could. This love she showed to Pali even when their relationship became unfriendly and hurtful. Borka especially loved their children but she also liked Covi. When Borka and Covi went shopping together, the shop owners were surprised to see "such a young grandma" as Borka was only eight years older than Covi but she treated her with motherly care. Thus, the small children might have thought of her as a grandmother. Both Covi and the children loved Borka and she loved both her mother and grandmother roles.

During those years the English Electric Co. gave Mommy a commission to take photos of the Banhida power lines and electric works. These photos were such a success that they were subsequently published in a book. It was a well-paid job; I think she received about 2,000 pengos from this job.

Typing commissions came to an end for Borka though Pali continued to earn a good income for years and could still afford a luxurious life, when a change occurred with Borka's photography work. According to a new order, museums could only commission the Hungarian News Agency (MTI) to take photos. In 1933 Borka was only allowed to photograph children. The notorious episode regarding 400 pengos occurred in 1934, during the time of Feri's [Borka's older brother, Dr Franz Alexander, noted psychoanalyst] second visit. Borka wanted to increase her photography work and asked Feri for a loan of 400 pengos, which she received from Annie [Feri's wife, Anita Venier Alexander, an artist and sculptor]. Buba already knows the details of the story, as I often told him.

Borka felt totally at ease when she was photographing children and as if she was in her element. The mothers were very satisfied with the photos and Borka was happy with the results. She took excellent photos and her little clients hugged her. Her income from this work increased year after year and in the later years, was considerable.

During those years we organised many social gatherings, first on Wednesdays and later it was changed to Thursdays. There were usually thirty to forty guests who were invited and we often served espresso coffee. During all of the evening get-togethers, we combined a lecture and a debate. The moderator was usually Imre Csecsy [1893–1961, MP, politician, and writer] yet I can also recollect a lecture given by Dr Gyuszi Engel [1844–1911, a physician], and the debate afterwards. I also remember Gisle Johnson's enjoyable lecture about Norway. I also gave a speech on Nietzsche and a musician named Bardos also gave an interesting lecture. Borka wanted to recreate the atmosphere of the Alexander household when she was growing up and organised these evening lecture courses. She often mentioned that their house was the centre of the spiritual and intellectual aristocracy of Budapest. All the lectures were successful and made Borka happy. Later on we hosted these evenings in the Cafe Modern in one of their many separate meeting rooms. But those lectures took place later than from 1931–35, in the years 1936–38.

I should also mention the Company of Individual Psychology, which I also attended, but ultimately it bored me. I gave one or two lectures there about Klager. I also gave a lecture on Klager at one of the cultural club evenings organised by Endre Nagy in the lounge of the Hotel Britannia. This lecture was quite successful. I also gave a speech on individual psychology and I was also grateful to speak on this topic as it was interesting to me. We spent many pleasant nights with Dr Kulcsar and his family until he separated from his wife and then we visited only with his estranged wife.

I had an accident on the River Danube when I was teaching Mrs Kartal's younger sister how to swim. She was frightened of the water and hung on to me so tightly that she almost pulled me under the water. Finally I managed to free myself from her grip and saved both of us. Though this sounds dramatic, it was an insignificant episode.

I should also mention that Borka travelled to the Netherlands in 1935. She took photos while she was gone and earned 2,000 pengos, which pleased her. Probably it was in this year that Lili and Aus came to see us in Pest and Lili behaved in a very strange manner. Interestingly, Aus tried to compensate for his former, notorious behaviour regarding the "pictures". I am not going to list the details here as this was also part of the "Pali complex". I can remember our having dinner on Janoshegy [in the Buda hills], where I first met Aus.

In the spring of 1935 Buba had pleurisy and he was ill in bed for six weeks. Luckily he recovered completely with Dr Katona's proper treatment and Borka's excellent care. There was not a nurse in the world like Mommy, full of love and kindness. Dr Katona had been our family doctor since 1933 and he was an outstanding and conscientious medical doctor and also a very honest man. Sadly, he was killed in the mass murders of 1944, after going to work in Germany. There was no trace of him after that. Sometimes I hoped that he might have escaped to Russia and might be able to come back home, but there is not much hope of that.

We arrive at the year 1936. Covi returned from Belgium without Pali and we spent, again, the holiday in Veroce together. At work, the Klein overtime-evening typing work reached a crisis. One afternoon he dictated a twenty-three-page letter for me, addressed to the General Electric Company in Buenos Aires, about organising an Argentinian branch of the Ganz factory. He demanded that the letter's translation be ready the following morning. I finished this work at 2.30 am and went home.

During these times I was so exhausted from working so much overtime that Borka insisted I go on a holiday to Italy. I did just that and travelled with an organised tour. Originally I wanted to meet Adolf and his family but that could not be arranged as I travelled instead to Mendola and the Savoy hills. I can recall the route very well, along Lake Balaton, to Trieste and Venice. It was as if the shade of past travels was flying next to me. But this trip felt somehow different and empty as Borka was absent. For me all the beauty in the world would have been richer with her by my side. I had to imagine those beautiful feelings generated by her vulnerable soul. She especially enjoyed the art, churches and buildings, paintings, and the statues in Venice. I could not enjoy the fine surroundings of Mendola without her; I was bored and homesick. I missed her more than usual.

In those days I had another accident, more serious than the one mentioned before, when I went for an outing with the daughter of an old friend, Valentin. I slipped on a stone and broke my arm. A rescue expedition was organised and I was taken back to my hotel. Only later did I receive medical help. A plaster cast was put on my arm, weighing twelve kilograms, which I had to wear for two months. I called Borka on the 27th of July and she thought I called to congratulate her on her birthday. She was shocked to hear the news of my accident. Adolf and Lilly came to see me in the hospital. I was only given permission to travel home after ten days. Mommy was waiting for me at Deli railway station and took me to Veroce where she cared for me and I made peace with the world because of her attention. Luckily I was on sick leave and was not required to return to work until the 15th of October although they sent me some translations to complete at home. Psychoanalysts told me that I caused the accident myself in order to escape the difficulties at work and I think, to some extent, it was true. Anyhow, the so-called tortures became somewhat easier after the 15th of October.

The war in Spain began in 1936, which was to be the forerunner to the later devastation. In Spain, Franco declared his "national" dictatorship. In Hungary Kalman Daranyi became prime minister and he soon passed his first anti-Jewish law in 1937. We were falling into a hole with such politicians as Bethlen, Gombos, and Daranyi [the right wing governments led by Gyula Gombos in the years between 1932 and 1936 and by Kalman Daranyi from 1936–38].

In the spring of 1937 I was again under a lot of pressure at the factory. We were required to complete an informative text about Ganz railcars for the Argentine business partner. That could have been accomplished in fifteen pages, but my boss, Mr Klein insisted on writing 105 pages which he dictated to me personally. Therefore, instead of taking merely three days, it took more than four weeks to complete. Because of this job, I could not join Borka and Buba who were leaving for Italy in the middle of June. I was set to leave in the middle of July when I handed the text to Klein in the lounge of the Hotel Ritz. I was only able to manage that because of the paid overtime. I was paid 1,000 pengos and, thus, I could cover the extra expense of the family holidays. Borka and Buba could stay in Italy for nine weeks, instead of the originally planned four or five weeks, and I could join them for about a month. We stayed in Fiumetto as paying guests in the house of Mark Vedres's daughter. Prior to my arrival, Mommy and Buba enjoyed a beautiful journey when they travelled to Assisi, Perugia, and Florence. We had lovely outings together, up into the hills to Massa, where Buba explored and I cycled. It was a beautiful summer, and ironically we then said farewell to the summers of the peaceful era. Next year, in 1938, the total European war threatened us though outright warfare was still delayed by the Munich treaty for a year. We stayed then in Abbazia and those times made up our last peaceful holiday despite its shortness.

In 1937, on the way home from Fiumetto, we went to see Adolf and then we travelled to Milan. There we visited the Dome. It was a beautiful summer. Mommy enjoyed the chance to show Buba all the beauties of art. In Eva Vedres's house there was good company. Her husband, Alberto worked as a lawyer and edited an antifascist journal with his friends. One of his friends was Ca'dorzi, a nobleman from Venice, and a Jew at the same time! Buba made friends with Alberto's nephew, Sampietro. Adolf came to see us and told us that the rooms and the food were free. There was a wonderful cook who served us Italian specialities. We enjoyed the sea, swimming, and we also went sailing. Borka had a very good time and everybody loved her. There were two children of friends and she also enjoyed their company. I felt five years younger during my four week long holiday spent with them. The nine week long holiday did a lot of good for both Borka and Buba. That year Borka was forty-five, I was fifty-three, and Buba was sixteen years of age. Buba had just finished the seventh form [year seven] that previous June. In 1937 we met Lili Brody. We were often invited by the family and spent one New Year's Eve together. I sympathised with her husband very much, yet at that time we did not recognise his severe mental illness which led to his ultimately committing suicide.

As far as I can remember we spent ten days in Abbazia at Christmas time. We stayed in a pension called Bristol and run by Dr Muller. It was there that we read the news of the tragic death of Dezso Czigany [1883–1937, painter]. Mommy was shocked by that news. We travelled home in the first days of January 1938.

CHAPTER FOUR

Nazism comes to Hungary

In 1938 the first wave of Nazism reached Hungary. In March 1938 the Anschluss of Austria took place. Just ten days later Mommy travelled to Vienna to see what might have happened to our friends and relatives who lived there. She went to see Zsofka and the Broessler relatives and experienced dreadful times that really shocked her.

On the 1st of April, 1938 Anna and Ili returned to us and in May a series of anti-Jewish laws was passed in Hungary. [Hungary was then ruled by Miklos Horthy and these anti-Jewish measures were meant to emulate Germany's Nürnberg Laws.] It is quite odd to say this now, but in 1938 we regarded this first twentieth-century Hungarian anti-Jewish law [Numerus Clausus] as simply amusing and grotesque but not dangerous. However, we thought that it would be better for Buba to attend an English university. He had already gained acceptance to Manchester University but he did not attend that university.

By the time 1938 began to draw to a close, an extreme wave of migration commenced because of the anti-Jewish laws. At the same time, I had a lot more interpreting work to do. In December I earned 2,000 pengos for my work including an additional 1,400 pengos salary for interpretations.

We still had our holiday in the autumn of 1938 in Abbazia [now Opatija, Croatia, a beautiful seaside village] and stayed again in the pension of Dr Muller. I can recollect a pleasant outing to a bay south of Abbazia. We had an exciting way back during a great storm. We went to see Medea, Morchiena where we did a lot of walking. We took an excursion to Monte Maggiore and to Schutzhaus. On the way home Mommy almost fainted in the car. Doctors told us that because of her high blood pressure she must avoid drastic changes in altitude. Therefore we never again exposed her to that. But no one could imagine that her high blood pressure would ultimately become fatal and cause our tragedy of losing her eight years later. I was frightened when this incident occurred and wondered what would happen to me if we had lost her then. But luckily she regained consciousness and we hoped that it would never happen again.

Of course I was aware of being mortal and I fantasised once that maybe, when I would be ninety years old and she eighty-two, both of us would die in the same second. I was sure it was impossible to live alone, without your spouse. I thought I could never endure such a situation as Borka meant life itself to me.

There was a small cafe nearby where we went to drink a cup of coffee every day. I so enjoyed having a coffee with her that it felt like a divine present though it was only coffee. The time I spent together with Borka brought me godlike happiness, and the time was also exciting. I enjoyed the beauty of the sea and the mountains a thousand times more with her as she gave meaning and value to everything. Often I went up the mountains alone as Mommy did not like going there, yet I nonetheless felt her presence during those times. The view from atop the hill, in the church, was spectacular and the view spanned to Chersora and Veglia.

Before we left, Adolf Polanyi came to see us and we said our farewells at the Fiume railway station. Who knew if we would ever meet again? World War II was to break out at any moment.

That summer Buba visited Pali and his family in England and on their way home they also travelled together to France and Switzerland by car. Pali and his family returned to England and Buba came home alone.

I did not spend much time with my brother Oszkar or his family. Our differing worldviews separated us, which was precipitated by their great wealth. I remember visits to their apartment which they rented in a villa on Stefania Road. The atmosphere was very depressed in their home and they had to be careful what they said or did as the German embassy was located just one floor above them. I also took care of my other brother, Ervin, in those years. He had just returned from Germany in quite a depressed mood because the Hitler regime had confiscated his shop. I remember our long conversations in the Cafe Modern during the evening hours when I tried to encourage him and cheer him up. Finally Oszkar managed to get a job at Leo Goldberger [1878–1945, a well-known manufacturer of textiles]. At the beginning he only had a modest post but in a year's time he received a leading position. I also asked for his assistance with translations and we worked together for six months for an employer on Tatra Street and translated a technological periodical which was published in four languages. It could have been in the summer of 1938 because I can recollect writing certain translations, which were part of this work, in Dr Muller's pension in Abbazia and we definitely stayed there in 1938.

In 1939 my interpretation work continued. We bought a new typewriter on the 2nd of January for 210 pengos and by that evening I had earned the equivalent of a usual day's income. Mommy also worked tirelessly. I often returned home from the factory around eleven o'clock at night but I had only to sign the documents as Mommy could work alone. We prepared secondary school final exam certificates, birth certificates, and other documents. Mommy could also, on her own, translate university students' examination certificates and, again, she followed the samples provided. Klari and Edit Wertheim helped her. I often signed the documents between 11 pm and 12.30 am.

We spent Easter 1939 in Lepence where we heard the news that Italy had invaded Albania. [Albania had long been of considerable strategic importance to Italy. Italian naval officers desired the special ports near the entrance to the Bay of Vlorë as such a coup meant Italy would control the entrance to the Adriatic. Italy also hoped that Albania would provide her with a foothold nearby in the Balkans. Interestingly, prior to World War I (1914–1918), the forces of Italy and the Austro-Hungarian Empire worked in concert to create an independent Albania and now Italy wanted to reverse that action. When World War I began, Italy took advantage of the chance to invade the south of Albania in order to avoid it being captured by the Austro-Hungarian troops. Italy's occupation did not last long and in 1920 Albania forced Italy to withdraw. Italy's military and Benito Mussolini were embarrassed by what had happened before, and saw the chance to invade in 1939 as payback and retribution for what took place years earlier. The Italian invasion of Albania (April 7–April 12, 1939) was a brief military campaign and Albania was rapidly beaten, its ruler went into exile, and Mussolini annexed that part of Albania and made it part of Italy.]

In 1939 Buba returned from Italy together with the Polish people. Earlier, in May Borka stayed in Abbazia in the Lakatos pension.

The outbreak of the Second World War took place on 1 September 1939 with the German invasion of Poland. At 4.45 am, some 1.5 million German troops invaded Poland all along its 1,750-mile border with German-controlled territory. Simultaneously, the German Luftwaffe bombed Polish airfields, and German warships and U-boats attacked Polish naval forces in the Baltic Sea. Nazi leader Adolf Hitler claimed the massive invasion was a defensive action, but Britain and France were not convinced. On 3 September, they declared war on Germany, initiating World War II.

To Hitler, the conquest of Poland would bring Lebensraum, or "living space" for the German people. According to his plan, the "racially superior" Germans would colonise the territory and the native Slavs would be enslaved. German expansion had begun in 1938 with the annexation of Austria and then continued with the occupation of the Sudetenland and then all of Czechoslovakia in 1939. Both had been accomplished without igniting hostilities with the major powers, and Hitler hoped that his invasion of Poland would likewise be tolerated.

Fearing imminent attack, Poland began to call up its troops but Britain and France persuaded Poland to postpone general mobilisation until August. To neutralise the possibility that the USSR would come to Poland's aid, Germany signed a non-aggression pact with the Soviet Union on 23 August 1939. In a secret clause of the agreement, the ideological enemies agreed to divide Poland between them. Hitler gave orders for the Poland invasion to begin on 26 August, but on 25 August he delayed the attack when he learned that Britain had signed a new treaty with Poland, promising military support should it be attacked. To forestall a British intervention, Hitler turned to propaganda and misinformation, alleging persecution of German-speakers in eastern Poland.

Buba was not admitted to Budapest [Pazmany] University in spite of his excellent high school grades and a recommendation by Kornis (certainly because the so-called numerus clausus [anti-Semite laws] law limited the number of Jewish students at every Hungarian university), so he worked as a labourer at Ganz dockyard during the 1938–39 school year. In the autumn of 1939 he was finally admitted to the University of Budapest. [The second anti-Jewish law of the Horthy regime was passed in May 1939.]

Now I realise that I have almost reached our twentieth year (1940) and I have not mentioned a lot of other things yet. Though not a moment of shared and enjoyed memories with Borka should be lost. I have not mentioned the little summer house of Karoly Pollacsek's [1886–1964, philosopher and politician] family at Uromhegy [near Budapest] where we spent many happy Sundays which made all of us, and especially Borka, very pleased. These Sunday meetings began in 1920 and went on until 1928 when poor Dr Karoly Pollacsek died. Later the meetings continued and were organised by his widow, until her death. Great times were had and good friends attended: Emil and Sandor Nemes and their families, the Gonczy family, the Vago and the Hollo families, sometimes Attila Jozsef [significant poet 1905–1937], Gyuszi Engel and his family, the Lederer family, and the Schilling family and many other friends. Borka always helped Mrs Pollacsek lay out the table and serve the food. She reflected good feelings to everyone as she sensed their fondness of her. We always sang a lot of songs. All of us were connected by the events of 1918 [revolution]. Karoly Pollacsek's best friend was Oszkar Jaszi and his cousin was Ervin Szabo [1877–1918, social scientist, director of the Budapest library which later was named Szabo Ervin Library]. The Polanyi boys, Misi, Karli, and Adolf [sons of Mihaly Polanyi] were also his cousins and were the embodiment of intellectuality. These three men remained abroad but we always heard news from them. These friendships and these meetings were a sort of asylum where one could forget about the reign of the counter-revolution in Hungary and we could hope for the chance of change. Many members of this group were freemasons and that also added to the feeling of fraternity among us. That was the real connection among us because there was no opportunity for political activity any more. We were waiting for a better time, but instead a much worse one came.

They were also fond of me, first of all because of my friendship and yearning for Adolf. Pollacsek always helped me and defended me during the shutting down of our company, Uzemgazdasag. Additionally, Mrs Pollacsek was grateful that I arranged for the English Electric Company to lease their flat on Maria Valeria Street. This lease paid quite a nice sum, annually 6,000 pengos, which greatly helped her financial situation.

Maybe that was why she remembered me in her will and left me some furniture. In the final years the Nemes family home became the centre or home base for our meetings. Buba often accompanied us, especially in those early years. Borka was loved by all of them and she was happy to feel their affection.

I should also mention Borka's relationship with Vera, her brother Paul's second daughter, whom she loved as a step-daughter. I think the feeling was mutual.

Even "old Aunt Cecil" loved Borka in spite of the fact that she usually did not like most people. Many people tolerated her only because of her children and because of her wits, yet were quick to criticise her amorality. She was regarded as "the grandma of the revolution". But her children did not like her very much because of her amoral personality when her house became the centre of this progressive company. I can remember one evening, when we also stayed there with Borka and with about eighty other people, among others Frigyes Karinthy [writer 1887–1937] and Dezso Kosztolanyi [writer, 1885–1936]. I can remember a dialogue between Karinthy and Kosztolanyi. Karinthy asked Kosztolanyi: "What sort of sports do you do nowadays, Dezso?" and Kosztolanyi answered unsuspectingly: "I usually go swimming." "Where exactly?" asked Karinthy. "In Rudas spa, though I do not like it very much," answered Kosztolanyi. "Naturally," reacted Karinthy, "because you cannot drift and swim with the current." Karinthy criticised Kosztolanyi for giving too many allowances to the reigning regime, but I think he exaggerated this. Aunt Cecil taught me Russian first and then I explained the Gospels to her. I can also remember a grand party given by her in a separate hall of Hotel Bristol and at least 120 people were invited. She had a suite in this hotel, which was her third apartment, and in the meanwhile she also stayed with the Pollacsek family for a time. And at the end of her life she lived at Eskü Square and she died there at the age of eighty-one. She often pulled Borka's leg, but she was also fond of her.

One of our closest friendships was with the Miklos Gimes—Lili Hajdu couple; Lili was certainly Borka's best friend. In the spring of 1923 a lipoma was found on Borka's breast that doctor Polya suspected to be cancerous. Borka required surgery and Lili stood next to Borka in the operating room and took her pulse. Fortunately the lump was not cancer. Lili Alexander [Borka's younger sister, the youngest of the Alexander-Broessler children] stayed in Pest at that same time to be baptised prior to her marriage to Edward von Saher but she did not come to see us and did not visit Borka in the hospital either.

I met the Gimes couple in 1918 at the Radical Party meetings and we often had dinner together afterward. They were one of the families, besides the Pollacsek and Polanyi families [the family changed its name from Pollacsek to Polanyi], whom I introduced Borka to after our wedding. The Gimes couple lived then on Uzsoki Street and they also participated in the Remetehegy meetings (when they lived there), together with the Szilagyi, Mignon, and the Czigany families. There were lots of bridge parties in our flat where I also learned to play the game but not well.

In the year of persecution, Lili told us if she had a flat we could also stay there. Borka just stayed at Lili's when we got the news that we could move to the Buda apartment of Elemer Pajzs [1894–1944, writer and journalist]. Buba always spent the summers in Remetehegy and enjoyed the company of the other children his age and they all socialised together. Borka was loved by every member of that group and she was also very fond of all of them. Zsigmond Kende's wife, Margit [Zsigmond Kende, and his wife, Margit, were both medical doctors, Zsigmond 1888–1971] loved Borka very much and the feelings were mutual. Unfortunately Margit died and as far as I can remember her burial took place in 1939. After the Remetehegy meetings we used to go to Szentendre to a small weekend house where we spent many happy Sundays and Borka often spent a week of her holidays there.

[Almost one half of all the Jews that were killed at Auschwitz were Hungarian Jews who were gassed within a period of ten weeks in 1944. Up until the spring of 1944, it had been the three Operation Reinhard camps at Treblinka, Belzec, and Sobibor that were the main Nazi killing centres for the Jews, not Auschwitz.

The order to round up the Hungarian Jews and confine them in ghettos was signed by Lazlo Baky of the Royal Hungarian government on 7 April 1944. Jews in Hungary had been persecuted since 1092 when Jews were forbidden to marry Christians.

The deportation of the Hungarian Jews began on 29 April 1944 when a train load of Jews were sent to Birkenau on the orders of Adolf Eichmann, according to the book by Laurence Rees. According to *The Holocaust Chronicle*, a huge book published in 2002 by Louis Weber, the CEO of Publications International, Ltd., another train filled with Hungarian Jews left for Birkenau on 30 April 30 1944; the two trains with a total of 3,800 Jews reached Birkenau on 2 May 1944. There were 486 men and 616 women selected to work; the remaining 2,698 Jews were gassed upon arrival.

On 8 May 8 1944, former Commandant Rudolf Hoess was brought back to Auschwitz-Birkenau to supervise the further deportation of the Hungarian Jews. The next day, Hoess ordered the train tracks to be extended inside the Birkenau camp so that the Hungarian Jews could be brought as close as possible to the gas chambers.

According to Laurence Rees, in his book *Auschwitz, a New History*, the first mass transport of Hungarian Jews left on 15 May 1944 and arrived at Birkenau on 16 May 1944. The mass transports consisted of 3,000 or more prisoners on each train.]

We also had good relationships with the Alexander and the Broessler relatives in Pest. There was an especially good relationship between Borka and "Tante Anny" [Aunt Anny], the mother of Iren and Lenke Broessler and Szabo Gabi, one of

Iren's daughters. During the years of hiding it was especially painful for Borka that she was unable to take care of Aunt Anny. Borka did not even know where she was and later on it was said that she died of starvation during the war.

Borka also stayed in touch with the Broesslers of Vienna and via Feri she managed to get an American visa for Guszti [Hungarian nickname for Gustav: Gustav Broessler was the first cousin to Feri (Dr Franz Alexander) and the father of Ruth and Eva who escaped the Nazis when placed on the Kinder Transport travelling from Vienna to Amsterdam]. Borka also visited Otto and his family after the Anschluss in Vienna and they still remember Borka with much love as I read in their recent letters. They wrote the following: "Borka differed from her sisters and brothers, namely she was mild and good, while her sisters and brothers were hard, rigid and egotists." Another lady, Klari Kiss also felt close to Borka and remembered her with kindness.

On 1 September 1939 with Germany's invasion of Poland and with France and England declaring war against Germany, World War II began. The Polish invasion and the ensuing battles ended in a few weeks with Poland's total and complete defeat and collapse; they expected the French and English to help, but in vain. England's help was only in the form of a naval blockade and the French had their policy of "drôle de guerre" [phoney war] where the armies faced each other but did not attack.

People who remained in Budapest were relatively calm and no one believed that Hungary would participate in this war. Horthy [the governor of Hungary 1920–1944] stated stupidly, "We feel empathy towards our German allies as well as towards our Polish brothers." Interestingly, the governor did not say how we could do that when the two opposing sides simply wanted to kill each other.

The two of us worked quietly. Then, after the 1st of January 1940 (and not 1939 as I wrote above), my interpreter work ended. Klein still remained at the Ganz factory (he would leave in the autumn of 1940), but his temperament softened somewhat. We spent our holiday again in Abbazia at Pension Lakatos [Lakatos is a Hungarian name; Abbazia used to belong to the Austro-Hungarian monarchy until 1918] during the spring of 1940 for the last time.

The war in Europe raged on during the summer of 1940: there was war in France, the Petain regime was established, and then the "Blitz" in London. The summer ended with the defeat of the German Air Force and the entry of Italy into the war. Mussolini wanted to take advantage of a defeated France. I recall that I bought many foreign newspapers from street vendors as the newspapers were freely available; Hungary was still neutral at this time.

In July 1939 Polanyi Misi sent me a letter and asked me to take care of Zsofka in Vienna because her husband had been taken to the concentration camp in Dachau. From then until her death in 1941, I looked after poor Zsofka as part of my everyday tasks. Until the spring of 1940 it seemed reasonable to help Zsofka with Misi's assistance, and we hoped that it may be possible to help Zsofka and even her husband get to America. We thought Karli and Mausi, already in America, could assist us. Cordell Hull, US secretary of state in the FDR administration, wrote a letter to the American consul in Vienna. But all these efforts were in vain and mostly because of Zsofka herself unfortunately.

There were some important changes in the Ganz factory: Feri [nickname for Franz, Ferenc in Hungarian] Klein emigrated to South America [probably in 1940], then the death of the old Gyula Klein [probably in 1941] who was the president, and finally the death of Bajer [probably in 1943]. I had much less work to do after Klein left and Hungary entered the war. I was still employed by the factory because everybody expected the defeat of the Germans and hoped that our contracts with the

British partners would be revived. Nobody expected the tragic events that led us to the German defeat.

I had no English translations in the period following 1941. That gave me the time to dictate letters to help with Zsofka's case while at work in the factory. Her husband perished in Dachau [Artur uses this term "perished" that is usually used in Hungarian regarding those who were killed in concentration camps; this is considered to be some sort of protective distancing defence mechanism to guard oneself from the actual cruelty of being killed] and then Zsofka was deported to Poland where her son was killed (for whom Mommy had previously managed to get a visa to San Domingo). After that I could only help members of Zsofka's family by sending them the permitted sum of 100 marks along with some clothes. The parcels were sent to Poland where she lived more than a year and a half until the autumn of 1941 when my postcard was returned saying "recipient's destination unknown". We knew at once what this meant. She was dead.

In the summer of 1940 we stayed in Lepence, but I am not sure if this date is correct. As far as I recall, the Szentpal group [Szentpal Olga 1895–1968, choreographer, dance and art of movement artist, her group of dancers was called the Szentpal group] performed *A Midsummer Night's Dream* next to a forest and maybe that actually took place in 1941. My memories of these years are not at all complete or dependable. There was a big group and new friends as well. Mrs Pikler, the wife of a medical doctor, and the couple who manufactured paper and had such a tragic fate in the year of persecution, were also present. Besides that I am reminded that a violinist called Rados, and a chess player, and a manufacturer called Miskolczy, and the girl whom he later married were present. These memories are from the summer of 1941. I can remember Buba's visit to Pecs [a city in south-west Hungary] for two days in the same year. We also a met a family whose one son was an art historian and many members of that family perished in the year of persecution. I cannot remember their name either.

Borka made friends easily and these summer weeks in Lepence were so beautiful! In spite of not having anything special to do in Lepence, she was present and that meant everything to me. While we vacationed in Lepence, the fighting between Germany and the Soviet Union broke out and Hungary was now implicated in the war.

I cannot remember anything of the year 1942. I know I went for a cure in Lukacs Spa [in Buda] for four weeks. In the autumn a good friend died. He was a professor and taught in a secondary school whose son was a famous mathematician in England, but I cannot recall their names. In 1942 Buba stayed in Parkanynana.

In March I was hit by a woman cyclist (later it became known that she was a fascist). She cycled while she was drunk and after she hit me, I fell to the stone pavement and suffered a skull fracture. The ambulance car took me to Korond Sanatorium. Mommy was staying with Nelly in Mecsek, and Buba went to meet her at the station and reported the news of my accident. She took a cab and was in a hurry to get to the hospital as soon as possible. She visited me daily, and after a fortnight she took me home. In three months I had totally recovered.

While I was in the sanatorium I heard the news of El Alamein [First Battle of El Alamein: 1–27 July 1942; Second Battle of El Alamein: 23 October–4 November 1942]. Later on I heard the news of the Allied invasion of Sicily [9 July–17 August 1943], and I had already heard about the Siege of Stalingrad [23 August 1942–2 February 1943]. We expected then that there soon would be a total victory by the Allies, but victory took a much longer time.

After my recovery Mommy spent two weeks in Szentendre at the house of the Gimes couple. In the autumn of that year I finished the dictation of the Schimanek translation in the factory; it took a year to complete. At the end of 1943 Borka began to participate in some Jewish charity work. There were programmes organised every two to three weeks and the admission fees collected at the door were sent to a Jewish aid programme. We often took part in these programmes.

I can remember many parties and at one party Erno Szep [writer 1884–1953] read some of his writings and Mommy helped everywhere she could.

The atmosphere in Budapest worsened and we could not hold the usual Thursday evening meetings as previously. During those years such a meeting of thirty to forty people would attract the attention of the police and they might intervene. Some of our friends still came to see us: Dr Katona, the Engels, and Ervin [his brother], who read us the news and "commentaries" regarding the war. The commentaries were written by those who expected an Allied victory and, therefore, tried to raise our spirits.

There had already been some air raids but only small ones. There were only two Russian attacks. We did not go to the air raid shelter then but watched the so-called "Stalin candles" (Soviet firebombs) from our window. Once I broke the blackout law accidentally when I lit a cigarette in the living room while looking down to the street below at one o'clock am. I was positive that the roller blinds were pulled down and I switched on the lights of the big chandelier. But the blinds were actually operating. The light was so bright that it could have been seen from the Buda Castle [located opposite, on the Buda side of the River Danube, from where Belgrade Street intersected the Elizabeth Bridge]. A policeman arrived immediately and we were frightened as I could have been taken away and imprisoned. I guess all that took place in November 1943. Happily we were lucky to narrowly escape real trouble and the police fined us a mere 120 pengos instead. Actually I am not really sure if this event took place in November 1942 or 1943 [the second time Artur acknowledges confusion regarding dates, perhaps a result of his skull fracture and concussion].

The air attacks became more frequent during 1944 as the Allies had an airbase in Italy and their planes took off from there; it was not that far from Budapest. At night it was mainly the English who attacked us while in the daytime it was the American air forces who attacked. A rumour was circulating, characteristic of anti-Semite foolishness, claiming that the Jews sent light signals to our enemies to help drop bombs. Another rumour of this kind was that the Allied forces threw down explosive bombs in the form of dolls and chocolate to kill children. All this insanity was believed by an ever enlarging and broadening layer of Hungarian society.

Our air raid shelter was quite primitive at first but people worked on it, step-by-step. In 1944 it became a part of our lives: awakening during the night, hearing the sound of the air raid signal, and walking down the dark staircase to the air raid shelter. Inside the shelter we tried to somehow pass the time by talking, reading, and eating until we heard the sound of the "air raid danger over" signal. The elevator then took us back up to our flat.

It was in 1944 when we were initially visited by Lili's first husband [not a legal husband], who was a film director, and lived here as a tenant in the house. We received him with the greatest affection but it seemed he did not want to reveal our intimate connection to the others while in the air raid shelter. Maybe he was fearful of the Arrow Cross regime that was becoming stronger in those days. He wrote an inflammatory journal article titled "We are alone" and, because of that, Mommy gave him a piece of her mind in a very dramatic scene when we were all in the air raid shelter together.

I should also remember to mention my sister, Irma. I took care of her during those (1938–1944) years, more intensively than earlier. Because of the anti-Jewish laws, her husband's income was reduced and she required financial assistance. Her two sons inherited a considerable sum but Irma would receive 1,000 pengos on two occasions and only because of my intervention. Her younger son supported her and gave her initially 100 pengos a month, later 300 pengos. My brother, who supported them for years, gave them regularly a monthly sum of 100, later 300 pengos. I also helped her with a monthly donation of 50 pengos plus food worth another 30–40 pengos, and gave her extra food as presents for her birthday and Christmas. Altogether they were able to have quite a good living by receiving all this financial support. I spent many pleasant afternoons in their home where I sang, mostly Schubert songs, and Irma played the piano. Irma respected and loved Mommy very much; Borka was always nice and good to her. She rarely accompanied me to Irma's but when she did, it was a feast for Irma. My sister cherished her as if she were a superhuman being. I could hardly convince Irma to come to see us as she had problems with her eyesight and was afraid to go home in the dark streets. When she did visit us, she had a good time. She wanted to leave her Bechstein piano to Buba in her will but I would not allow it. I think I was right to say no. There was a complicated lawsuit later regarding her will and I did not want to get Buba involved in such unpleasantries.

And then we come to the most dangerous and dramatic date of 19 March 1944 when German forces marched into and occupied Hungary (Operation Margarethe). The previous day, 18 March was a Saturday, and Maria, who lived in one of our rooms as a tenant, rushed into our part of the flat around 5 pm saying, "German troops marched into Hungary, they are approaching from the direction of Huvosvolgy!" [a district in Buda].

[The Hungarian prime minister, Miklos Kallay, with the knowledge and approval of Regent Miklos Horthy, had been discussing an armistice with the Allies. Adolf Hitler learned about these secret meetings and believed that the Hungarians had betrayed him. On 12 March 1944 he ordered his troops to initiate Operation Margarethe to capture critical Hungarian facilities.

Hitler invited Horthy to the palace at Klessheim, just outside Salzburg on 15 March. As Hitler and Horthy seemingly were discussing options, Germany's troops quietly moved into Hungary. The meeting was merely a trick to assure Horthy's absence from Hungary and to leave the Hungarian Army leaderless. Negotiations between Horthy and Hitler continued until the 18th when Horthy boarded a train to return home to Budapest.

When Horthy arrived in the capital city, German soldiers were already there, ready to greet him. Horthy was told that Hungary could only remain sovereign if he removed Kallay and installed a government that would fully cooperate with Hitler. If Horthy did not remove Kallay, Hungary would be occupied immediately. Horthy appointed Dome Sztojay prime minister to appease Germany. The occupation was a complete surprise, quick and bloodless. Soviet forces were advancing from the north and east, the British and American forces would soon invade the Balkans, and Germany decided to retain the Hungarian army forces, and sent some forces to defend the passes through the Carpathians.]

My immediate answer was disbelief: [using the formal invocation] "Oh, please don't believe these mad tales, they are surely rumoured by the Arrow Cross [Hungarian fascist] people. Why on earth would German troops march into Hungary? They are already here anyway. Their reliable people sit at desks at railway stations, offices, and post offices everywhere. Maybe there are just four Red Cross or other ambulances to Saint John Hospital [at the bottom of Huvosvolgy Road] and the Arrow Cross people call it an invasion to frighten people."

Unfortunately, the next day we learned that Maria was right. Seemingly all of Budapest was taken over by German soldiers. A deadly silence hung over the city. The Hotel Astoria became the German headquarters and the Hotel Royal became their main accommodations. And German tanks rumbled everywhere.

We just gazed at this awful scene in numbed silence. How could German troops do all that to our country? Was there no resistance at all? Where was the Hungarian Army? Where was the governor of Hungary? They were nowhere to be seen. The German invasion took place without any resistance. The Hungarian Army as well as the governor cowardly humbled themselves [to Hitler's demands]. A majority of members of the Hungarian Army were even happy with this outcome. While he had done nothing to save the Jews of the countryside, Admiral Horthy, Hungary's ruler, stopped the deportation of the Budapest Jews, at least until he was overthrown by the Arrow Cross, the Hungarian Nazis, in October 1944.

I myself really did not understand what had happened: Germany initiates a mad war against the world, in which they will undeniably be defeated soon. The war against Russia is far away, out on the Russian plain. Why do they need to invade Hungary in the process? They had already occupied our railway lines and all supply routes for a long time. This made no sense at all from a military point of view.

I could not imagine what their reasoning was other than to invade the country to kill one million Hungarian citizens, owing to their crazy beliefs about Jews and to sack all the rural areas in the meantime. It was impossible to do anything individually. We could only trust in the Allied forces' quick victory and that as a consequence the Germans would back off. Trust in this! That was what I did.

My optimism did not leave me. I think this could have been what is called faith in God in the age of the Bible. Because belief is not equal to a theological view. It did not mean that "to believe in the existence of God, preached by priests, in spite of the statements of the atheist scientific view". This would not have any sense in the age of the Bible. First of all no atheist scientific view existed to be contradicted. On the other hand the idea of faith in the existence of God was such a fundamental idea in the biblical worldview as is the idea of "Nature" in the natural sciences nowadays. Denying the existence of "Nature" nowadays would have been as senseless as denying the existence of God in the biblical worldview.

A large number of Hungarian doctors, lawyers, engineers, writers, musicians, and artists during these times between the two wars were identified as Jews.

Their success was intolerable for certain quasi-patriotic nationalistic political leaders in Hungary. Following the great loss of land and status after World War I, Jews remained a visible minority in Hungary and the target for easy discrimination. Jews were targeted and identified as a scapegoat for all that happened after World War I. Anti-Jewish policies were reinstituted after a period of relative acceptance and the Arrow Cross party began to enrol many followers. Hungary's leaders hoped to gain lost territories and in so doing sided with Germany and Italy who would take Hungary's side. During the war Jews were sent to the front lines to clean up minefields without protection and were also sent to labour camps (as was Alfred Renyi) in Germany. More than 15,000 Jews from Budapest were killed in such labour camps. In spite of that, Hungary resisted Germany's attempt to deport Jews to Auschwitz until March 1944, when German troops invaded Hungary.

The relocation of Budapest's Jews was the second stage of the Hungarian Holocaust. By this time, in 1944, more than 300,000 Jews had been deported from the countryside to Auschwitz. Women, children, and the elderly were gassed on arrival. Others were sent to Germany to be used as slave labour, as mentioned above. None of this could have happened without the willing cooperation of the Hungarian state, especially the brutal gendarmerie.

On 15 May 1944 the first trains left for Auschwitz. It was already near the end of the war, and even though Eichmann and his staff knew that Germany by now had lost the war, trains continued to roll into Auschwitz. Between 15 May and 9 July 1944, according to German records, 437,000 Hungarian Jews were deported. Between 1940 and 1945, one million Jews were murdered there and every third victim was a Hungarian. Additionally, back in the capital, the Arrow Cross militia shot and killed 10,000 to 15,000 Jews. Many of these executions took place on the banks of the icy Danube in the winter months of 1944–45. Jews were rounded up from the yellow star homes and other residences and taken to the river's edge. They were told to remove their shoes and were shot on site and their bodies fell forward into the river effortlessly. By the time the Budapest ghetto was liberated on 16 January 1945, almost fifty per cent of the city's Jewish population had been killed in the Holocaust.]

Some days later we received the yellow star decree. [On 16 June 1944, the mayor of Budapest, Akos Dorogi Farkas, issued a decree that marked out almost 2,000 apartment buildings in Budapest, "in which Jews (obliged under the existing decrees to wear the mark of the yellow star) may reside". Every one of these apartment buildings had to "… mark all their street entrances with a yellow star which must be kept permanently intact and clean. The sign shall be a six-pointed canary yellow star measuring 30 centimetres in diameter, on a 51 × 36 cm black background."] If this decree was to make Christians aggressive against Jews, it did not work in the first few days. Most people looked at the victims of this silly brutality with respect and empathy. People stood up on the tram and gave their places to those who wore yellow stars. [That is an observation unique to Artur, other survivors tell just the contrary.]

I wore the yellow star on my overcoat on my way to Ganz in the early days and while in the office I put the same yellow star on my shirt. Soon we were warned by Cross Arrow members of the secretariat that the office was a public place so we needed to wear an additional star on our jacket as well. So we did that. Anyhow, I thought, this will surely come to an end in a couple of days, on the day when they realise what mad idiocy it all is! Of course, we were disappointed because it did not end soon.

Meanwhile we were listening to the BBC radio from England, and on some days the radio from Moscow, and that helped to keep our hopes alive. The first awful blow happened on the 6th of June: Buba was called up for labour service. My optimism was gone and as I said farewell to him, I wept. But I tried to regain my former optimism and hoped that he would soon return safely.

We let one of our rooms to a colleague of Buba's, a mathematician who was terminally ill. Naturally he was pessimistic and I can remember explaining it to Renee that this poor man is only pessimistic because that will ease his suffering and that was true. But unfortunately his pessimistic prognosis proved to be true.

The second attack hit us on 22 June: we were forced to leave our flat near the Elizabeth Bridge overlooking the Danube for a house marked by a yellow star. [The yellow star homes numbered nearly 2,000 and were selected as compulsory residences for Budapest Jews from 21 June 1944 until late November 1944. The idea was that by housing the Jews in easily identifiable places, when it was time for them to be taken to the ghetto and then on to Auschwitz, it would be easier to round them up.] Our flat had been Borka's home for forty-one years and mine for twenty-four years. Leaving was really awful, especially for Borka. Only her studio remained there. But this is all for a short period of time and we can soon return, I thought. Unfortunately, this hope did not come true. We never got this flat back even after our liberation, for many reasons. Reasons that included damage from the bombings, a roof that required renovation, and so on.

Meanwhile, I forgot to say that I was laid off from the Ganz works on the 1st of May for six months. That meant they did not need my work but I received a cancellation-salary for six months plus a dismissal payment also equal to six months' salary, paid to me monthly. I thought we would be financially secure for twelve months and I believed that the war would be over by then, the Germans would be gone, and so would the anti-Jewish laws. That outcome actually happened, but not without tragedy beforehand.

So back to the 22nd of June 1944: we needed a new flat. We planned to move in with Lili [Lili Hajdu], however her house was not branded with a yellow star, and because of that, she also needed to find another place. We tried to find new flats, but they were all unsuitable. During the house hunting process we nearly became victims of a dishonest woman who collaborated with the murderers [fascists?]. I managed to prevent that from happening. I got up much earlier than necessary, collected information about her, and when it turned out that she lied to us, I cancelled our plan to rent from her. Divine providence saved us, or, to use a more modern phrase, an intuition which originated in our subconscious minds saved us.

We had pleasant memories of a New Year's Eve (in 1942 or '43) we spent in the home of Lili Brody. I suggested to Borka that we should ask them if it was possible for us to move into their home. Borka went to see Lili but she was twenty minutes too late, as Lili had already promised Mrs Arpad Pasztor that she could stay with them. Instead Lili promised to look for another place for us.

We were walking on, looking for flats but all of them were in terrible condition. The Pajzs family's flat seemed to be the best option for us even though fourteen people had already moved in. We could still be accommodated there, but we would have to settle for a small room. Finally we managed to receive a separate room in the flat of the Portuguese press attache, Elemer Pajzs. He, as a press attache, was not obliged to receive anybody in his apartment but as Lili Hajdu had asked him, we were permitted to stay. The two of us had a nice separate private room, while in those days usually four or six or eight Jews lived together in every room.

Borka and I arranged the necessary formalities with the Central Jewish Council people who were quite helpful in organising these moves. The Germans wanted to simplify the deportation of Jews and the Jewish organisations did not do anything to stop it. Their leaders, who were given protective passes by the Gestapo, were prepared to carry out the separation and registration of their fellow believers. It is an awful idea, but one must raise the question and ask, did they actually have a choice?

After that we moved into an attractive room with a similarly nice view of the Danube and the Buda hills like our old flat on the Ferencz Jozsef embankment had. We made friends with the Pajzs couple who hosted us and who were enjoyable people. The wife was an angelic person and full of goodwill. Pajzs had worked for the Portuguese embassy for four years to develop Hungarian-Portuguese cultural connections and was appointed to the post of press attache. We were just waiting for Buba to return home and we were happy to have the opportunity to stay in the Pajzs apartment.

The streets of Pest were in a terrible uproar during the days between the 22nd and 26th June, the days of our move. One quarter of Pest's inhabitants who were Jews, about 250,000 people out of one million, were forced to leave their flats and move into extremely crowded mass accommodations. Streets were filled with wagons fully packed with people's most necessary furniture, bedding, and other cherished belongings. The truckers/hauliers charged exorbitant fees, as much 1,000 pengos, to the desperate people. Misery could be felt everywhere. It was an apocalyptic scene. The impossible had happened. And later, even more impossible events took place.

The brief happiness we felt, because of our momentary reprieve, disappeared early on the evening of 26 June when further restrictions were imposed. Street posters made us aware that we, as Jews, were captives in our new homes. We were not allowed to leave home at all. Soon we were allowed to leave our flat between 10 am and 2 pm and only to buy food, visit a doctor, or go to a public bath and get washed. On Sundays we could not go anywhere; doctors' offices, shops, and public baths were closed. We were totally trapped. The way we were treated was inhuman.

We were anxiously waiting for our landlords (the Pajzs couple) to return home but they never arrived. We learned the next day that they were granted political asylum by the Portuguese embassy. They had learned that the perceived safety of the yellow star houses was only temporary.

It would remain Pest's eternal shame that these yellow star house decrees were put into force. It meant stigmatising 250,000 people, one quarter of all of the inhabitants of Pest. We should consider that only a much smaller portion of the 750,000 Christian inhabitants were educated at secondary school level compared to nearly all of the Jewish people. Therefore it meant stigmatising about one half of the educated inhabitants. What a terrible servility and vileness for putting this decree into force. All the members of the Christian population were merely puppets. No resistance was seen anywhere. Unfortunately, there was not any resistance on the part of the Jewish community either. As I have already mentioned, the leaders of the Jewish community also served this evil spitefully. The vilest instincts got out of control: envy, a wish to rob, and heartlessness. I would never have imagined that people could behave as they did. And one could not find a good, honest, heroic, or humane being. I saw neither resistors nor leaders. We received updated news stories of the deportations from cities all over the country. We did not know then that these people were carried off to gas chambers. But we heard that forty to fifty of them were crowded into carriages, including women, babies, and old people. Were there no priests, no servants of Christ, who could have stepped in front of the gendarmes with a cross in their hands to stop their villainous deeds? The members of the Hungarian "gentry" class sat in the ministries and edited and registered and put the murderous decrees into force. And what about the glorious "common folk"? Was it any better?

No, they just provided the Arrow Cross a mob who enforced the decrees. We had every reason to feel desperate.

In spite of all that we could manage not to be despairing. The monstrosity of it all made it totally absurd so, at the same time, it was easier for us to tolerate it all. After a time, we were permitted to leave our flat between 10 am and 5 pm and nobody monitored our movements if we went to see a doctor, bought food, or went for a bath or anywhere else. In the house where we were staying, people began to meet and make friends, even some bridge parties were held. We felt we could survive all of this and hoped that it would last only a few more weeks.

In the meantime we received good news about Buba. His forced labour squadron was a relatively good one; he himself did not suffer any personal Jewish-related insults. We were able to send him packages, most of which he actually received. Later on he was taken to Hajdunanas, where his situation worsened. He was forced to work in an airport building, in the midst of constant air raids, one of which destroyed all his personal belongings. However, he himself survived, was healthy, and the end of the war seemed near. His letters meant a lot to us and brought us pleasure.

I am a little embarrassed to confess that being together with Borka meant constant happiness for me even under those terrible circumstances. I stayed with her and that was happiness for me. I was even happier staying with her on this lonely island than in the quieter, peaceful days.

Borka continued to work in her studio at the Ferencz Jozsef embankment flat and she also worked as the head of a handicraft firm. She went there every day, took passport photos, and earned money. I also received my layoff salary from the Ganz factory and they also sent me translations because their new translators did not have adequate language skills. Their work had to be done by me and for this I received half of my previous income.

Then we wrote an application to obtain an exemption from the decree regarding Jews, invoking the legacy of Bernard Alexander, Borka's father. Such an exemption could have been granted by the governor. One of the tenants in the house, Maria Ronay, helped us complete the application. We also enclosed an attachment that we thought could not be refused. The Cultural Ministry tried to delay the matter, but finally we were informed that our application was sent to the governor's office. Unfortunately, the Arrow Cross people in his office sabotaged our application. I learned this from a former colleague who said that the Arrow Cross members working in the governor's office set aside the signed and approved documents.

The Pajzs family's flat had three rooms; we were given their bedroom, one of the rooms was closed off, but we could also use their study. There was a rich library and a desk with all the necessary items: collected sheets of paper, cigarettes, and so on, as if they had prepared for a long battle. We were given the keys to the desk and were asked to look after it all and save it, just in case other people moved in with us. Inside one of the books there was the menu card from one of their sea travels. We amused ourselves; Borka renamed our poor food using the names on the elegant menu list. We actually felt as if we stayed on a ship: even though the ship was at sea and was sometimes rocky, we felt safe and as though the ship would take us to a safe port in a few weeks.

They could trust us and we actually handed them everything when they returned prior to the time when others moved in. They took away everything with them and only a few of their books were left behind. Unfortunately, during these days, when Budapest was occupied, the Pajzs couple perished. They were carried off one night from the Buda villa belonging to the Portuguese consul. The Arrow Cross militiamen burst into the air raid shelter at the consul's house. Nobody saw the Pajzs couple again. Their seventeen-year-old son had disappeared earlier.

The Portuguese embassy gave us a strict order not to allow any strangers into the flat and we had to obey this command. If not, the Pajzs couple would get into trouble and we would also be sent away. But sometimes we kept people there for several days, if we thought that their lives could be saved that way. There was a famous pianist and her husband, a physicist, who were mistreated and spent four days with us before finding their own safe shelter. We provided shelter for another lady as well, who had been hiding in a monastery previously for a month but had to leave. She stayed with us until she could find sanctuary elsewhere. We also provided a place of refuge to my sister-in-law, Ila, for weeks at a time. In order for us to be able to say she was with us for only a few days' time, she rotated from our flat to another place often. We managed to acquire a room for my niece and her little daughter in our same building. This meant we could be together as a family during the day. When the Pajzs couple returned, we confessed to them that we had disobeyed their rules and they were very understanding.

The weeks and months passed this way and we received news about the deportation of Jews in the rural areas of the country. The threat of the deportation of the Jewish people of Pest continued. There was a moment of imminent danger when Maria Ronai told us that the Jews staying in a neighbouring street were carried off to be deported. We did not want to believe this though it would have happened to us if President Roosevelt, the Swedish king [Gustaf V], and the pope had not intervened.

[Just before the deportations began, two Slovakian Jewish prisoners, Rudolf Vrba and Alfred Wetzler, escaped from Auschwitz and handed the Slovakian officials papers outlining what was actually happening inside the concentration camp. This document, known as the Vrba-Wetzler Report, was quickly translated into German and distributed among Jewish groups and then to the Allied officers. Details from the report were broadcast by the BBC on 15 June and printed in *The New York*

Times on 20 June (Rees, Laurence, *Auschwitz: A New History*, Public Affairs, 2005). World leaders, including Pope Pius XII (25 June), President Franklin D. Roosevelt on 26 June, and King Gustaf V of Sweden on 30 June (A holokauszt Magyarorszagon: A deportalasok leallítasa (in Hungarian; retrieved 11 September 2006)), begged Horthy to use his influence to stop the deportations. Roosevelt specifically threatened military retaliation if the transports continued. On 2 July, Allied bombers executed the heaviest bombings inflicted on Hungary during the war. Hungarian radio accused Jews of guiding the bombers to their targets with radio transmissions and light signals, but on 7 July Horthy at last ordered the transports halted (Szita, Szabolcs, *Trading in Lives?* Central European University Press, Budapest, 2005, pp. 50–54). By that time, 437,000 Jews had been sent to Auschwitz, most of them to their deaths (Rees, Laurence, *Auschwitz: A New History*, Public Affairs, 2005). Horthy was informed about the numbers later: "approximately 400,000". By most estimates, one in every three people murdered at Auschwitz between May and July 1944 was a Hungarian Jew (Wilkinson, Alec, "Picturing Auschwitz", *New Yorker Magazine*, 17 March 2008, pp. 49–51).]

One day Borka met the always well-informed Mrs Madarassy who told her that she heard that Jews were to be sent out of the country to be killed and that the Christians would be taken away to do forced labour.

This news seemed to be authentic but it was not true. Religion did not make any difference to those making the decisions. Those who were deported and taken abroad were killed regardless of their religion. Those who were spared were also randomly chosen irrespective of their religion. But, at that time, we did not have this information and baptism seemed crucial in order to save our lives. For me it made no difference as I had already been baptised in 1908. All I had to do was to go to the parish and ask for my baptismal certificate. There was no problem since the Catholic Church prohibited anyone from leaving the Church. For Borka the process was more difficult. Jewish people could be baptised after paying a 1,000 pengos fee to the Buda parish. We did not have that much money then and, with Maria Ronai's help, we borrowed the money from Geza Supka [1883–1956, writer]. When Borka went to the parish office she found out that these sorts of quick baptisms were forbidden. Later on, I returned to the Jewish faith and in 1918 I also formally returned to the Jewish community.

We then turned to Kornis who was again helpful and suggested a Franciscan monk who could baptise Borka. The only problem was that this monk insisted that Borka first study the Bible for a period of three to six months. Borka said, "I am sorry, I do not have that much time," and the monk answered her with the following, "No problem, my lady, if you want to be a member of the Christian community, you are already in the state of 'being a wishful-Christian person'. If you were to be killed, you would receive the same treatment in the other world as if you had been baptized." Borka immediately left him but finally we managed to find a house on Tatra Street where the 200 tenants of the house could be baptised by a priest in a month. Each tenant had to pay 300 pengos. We could afford that sum and that meant we could return the former loan to Supka.

Meanwhile the Romanian government withdrew from the war. We expected Hungary to do the same but waited in vain. The Lakatos government was installed [the right wing government led by Geza Lakatos between August and October 1944] and it was followed by the actions taken by Roosevelt, the pope, and by the Swedish government previously mentioned. Finally the 15th of October arrived when Horthy issued a general order and announced Hungary's withdrawal from the war. I was very happy. I embraced the women in the house and thought that finally the persecution of Jews had come to an end. But my happiness was short-lived. Horthy's orders were announced on the radio but this was immediately followed by another announcement of quite a different tone. The second statement was totally contradictory to the first one. What really happened was that the Arrow Cross party had carried out a military coup d'etat and had also occupied the building of the Hungarian radio. The Hungarian "gentlemen" hurried to denounce Horthy, their former idol, and aligned themselves with Szalasi, the leader of the Arrow Cross party. There was actually no peace at all and the situation tragically worsened. An Arrow Cross dictatorship, led by Szalasi, was established. From then on, neither the exemptions issued by the former governor or given by the foreign embassies were valid. There were only about 300 exemptions remaining that Szalasi was willing to sign.

Our flat immediately lost its exempt status and, as a result, a real incursion of people took place. By the evening of the 16th of October 1944, sixty-one Jews were housed in our three rooms and, naturally, the sealed off room was also broken into. Twelve of the sixty-one people were later taken away to other places, leaving forty-nine behind. Borka invited some of her friends and some other women into our small room. Fifteen of us slept there and I was the only man among fourteen women. Borka became the "commander" of the flat and everybody willingly obeyed her. She cooked for our group of fifteen people while the others cooked for themselves.

A great event took place just before all of this happened. We were waiting for Buba's letters. We worried about him in spite of his writing optimistic and encouraging words. Then, all of a sudden, our doorbell rang and there he was—Buba. He had escaped from his forced labour squad. They were in a group, to be taken westward, at the railway station in Vac, when Buba just quietly slipped away from his troop, took the train to Pest, and travelled home.

Of course, his physical condition was not good. His hands and feet were covered with wounds. Borka put him to bed in the sealed middle room, the key to which we managed to acquire. Meanwhile she hung the second copy of the Portuguese ambassador's protective pass on the door. Buba's presence was naturally kept secret and he was not allowed to be seen by anyone. It was a great happiness that he could stay with us. Apart from small problems he was mainly well and safe. We never gave up hope and God showed us we were right to do so.

Everything was turned upside down by Horthy's failed attempt and by the Arrow Cross forces' coup d'etat. The Arrow Cross did not respect the exemption issued for our Portuguese flat. The house attendant informed us that everyone must go to the air raid shelter in the cellar and Borka left Buba locked in the sealed middle room. The house attendant informed us that if anyone was found upstairs he or she would be shot dead immediately. Borka instantly ran upstairs. Buba is upstairs! He must come down as it is surely more dangerous upstairs.

Buba did come down to join us in the queue in the courtyard, but a couple of minutes later he managed to escape in the midst of Arrow Cross followers and the police. He escaped using his unique skills and there began his life of illegality. He would later save my life and Borka's life combining his skills all the while, breaking the law.

We were taken into custody and placed in a yellow star house at 8 Visegradi Street. Raids were held again, searching for women aged 40 or under and men sixty and under. I was sick in bed. Borka was asked by them, "How old is your husband?" She answered perfectly calmly: "He is sixty-one." Should she have told the truth that I was sixty, I would have undoubtedly been taken away. [See also in Kertész Imre's Nobel prize awarded novel, *Fateless*, that the routine was the same in concentration camps; that boys under sixteen were killed and if they lied they were already sixteen, they were taken to forced work.] So I was left there. I turned to Borka, saying: "My dear Borka, with these words you saved my life again."

And it was not only my life that she saved. There was a young woman in our house with her three-year-old son called "little Gabi" who often stayed with us previously at the Pajzs's house. Borka decided to save this woman along with her son as she was less than forty years old and would most likely be taken away. I also helped as I was the one to stand as a guard at the house gate to identify the moment when our brute of a house caretaker was not there. I ran up to tell the woman: now. And she really was able to escape. Borka had previously taken this little boy away in her arms. The henchmen arrived and interrogated Borka as she had been seen with the boy. "Yes," she said, "I took him down to his mother. I don't know any more of him since that time." Both of them are still alive and well.

In the meantime we heard the news that the house of the Pajzs's flat was to receive a Swiss certificate signifying protected status and we could return if we had a personal Swiss Schutz Pass. [Raoul Wallenberg invented a special Swedish passport, the Schutz Pass. It was a colourful, imposing, official-looking document. With permission from no one, he announced that it granted the holder immunity from deportation to the death camps. Wallenberg distributed his Schutz Pass indiscriminately to Jews. The Schutz Pass alone is credited with saving 20,000 Jewish lives.] Our attempts to get one had been unsuccessful after many weeks of trying. And at that point Buba arrived and brought us a Swiss Schutz Pass. He was successful in obtaining one by taking a most dangerous chance. This was the first example of our being saved by Buba.

Borka wanted to save my sister-in-law, Ila, so she also typed Ila's name on our Schutz Pass. And so it began. Borka saved at least 200 people from death. She typed the wife's name where only the husband's name appeared. She also filled in blank Schutz Pass certificates. She behaved like a real protecting angel of all our community, risking her own life on every occasion.

Finally after three days of uncertainty the house of the Pajzs's flat actually did receive Swiss protection and so we went back to our former place using the Schutz Pass that we received from Buba. This time we were not alone as this was when the flat was turned into accommodations for many. We shared those three small rooms with forty-nine other tenants. It is almost impossible to describe how heroically sound and loving Borka was during those difficult days. She became the commander of our flat and everybody was always keen to obey her as people could feel all that goodness and love that flowed to us from her every single word. How rare this good spirit was in our world! How empty this world is now without her!

A difficult period followed. Raids continued every two or three days on the pretext of checking whether our Schutz Pass was valid or not. Fortunately it was impossible to confirm this and, unfortunately, people were carried off, chosen by chance. My sister-in-law, Ila, was almost carried off during such a raid in spite of the fact that our Schutz Pass was actually signed by the Swiss consul. That time Borka had already been sent to the safe side during the sorting process, however, she left the safe side to save Ila, and called out to the henchman with incredible heroism. I can't find words to describe it. Borka demanded Ila be let out as her name was also on our valid Schutz Pass that was accepted. She managed to get it done and, so, Ila's life was saved.

I cannot even describe all the daily events that took place. Once an Arrow Cross henchman took me away in order to bring me to their house of torture. I was able to make him feel merciful by saying some humane words. He then himself returned me to my relatively "safe" home. When I was almost taken to a forced labour camp, and could miraculously escape from the side of the road where people assembled, I had to thank a kind-hearted policeman and his pickpocket assistant who were surrounded by a mass of harlots. I recalled how my old friend Gisle Johnson cited Jesus's phrase from the Gospel telling the Pharisees "The publicans and the harlots go into the kingdom of God before you." And also another example when I met a drunk Swabian [of German ethnicity in Hungary] who possessed real wisdom and humanity. His humanity was suppressed by fascism and became released by alcohol, and so he gave us such an intelligent and humane speech that we hadn't heard for a long time in Hungarian so-called "elite company".

Buba could see that our lives had become more and more threatened by the continuing Arrow Cross raids so he told us to escape from our imprisonment. So we escaped. We succeeded in leaving the house while fifty policemen, in the middle of a raid, surrounded us. I will never forget that the distance between our side of the road to the edge of a "free" (but how dangerously free) world was only six metres. Buba was the one who saved our lives. He helped us escape. However, it would also have been impossible without Borka's heroism. I always had enough courage to go anywhere when I was in her company. Without her, I would have simply died.

Days of hiding followed our escape and we stayed in a flat at Dembinszky Street using the false documents Buba obtained with the help of his cousin Peter. Death was waiting for us on every street corner. People in the house suspected our true identity but Buba protected us by his bold appearance. By that time he had already worn a stolen military uniform with corporal stripes. His heroism was also legendary. Fifteen times a day he endured an identity check, but he always found his way back to us, to take care of us, and he helped us a thousand times. Then the siege began, bombs fell, and yet we somehow remained unconcerned. We were not afraid of death that might be the result of the bombs, no matter how dangerous they were, because they somehow meant less danger for us.

[Artur's change in style is quite meaningful: his sentences are many times a long list of events instead of using grammatically well-composed shorter sentences when describing those days of horror.] And also Christmas, presents from Buba, a festive dinner with walnut brandy and happy celebrations, and meanwhile the siege raged, aeroplanes bombed us, and there were bombs falling down, and roaring cannons around! A bomb explosion at our lichthof [a tiny, one or two square metre inner court of a many-storeyed house used only to supply some source of light and fresh air for toilets], a bomb falling on the opposite house that burst into flames, settling of German soldiers in our house, our peregrination from the second floor to the first one and later to the ground floor, and then to another flat at the ground floor and then back. Our landlady had pneumonia and Borka and Renee were taking care of her, Borka all day long, and they succeeded in healing her! This old lady cried so much at Borka's burial ceremony. "I, being seventy-five years old and had my life saved by Borka, am still here, and she had to go!" she cried. And that was also what I felt. How happily would I have died for her! And now I have to live without her!

CHAPTER FIVE

Liberation, at last

And then liberation, the Russians came on the 14th of January 1945. They broke into a wine cellar opposite us and gave wine to people. Buba also received ten litres in a large cauldron and we shared it with the other people in our house. This glass of wine—this was the signal of liberation.

So we reached the actual day of liberation, the 14th of January 1945. [During the siege of Budapest the Soviet Army took over the city from the Germans, marched on and fought day-by-day, house-by-house between December 1944 and February 1945. Almost every street had its own day of liberation. Liberation Day for Pest was 18 January, 13 February for all of Budapest, and 4 April for Hungary.] And now I still have to tell the story of the next nineteen months and eight days, until 22 August 1946, when our happy world collapsed.

Nineteen months—amid the most severe conditions; but still happy nineteen months. The last eight days were not, as those already meant that the catastrophe was approaching.

We came up from the cellar and saw a ruined town surrounding us with collapsed houses, empty shops with closed roller shutters, and a lack of food and other vital and basic necessities of life. All the bridges were blown up. Borka considered the loss of the bridges particularly painful as her inner self was so closely rooted to this landscape and this town. She especially missed the Elisabeth Bridge that arched over the river Danube, only a "brave jump" from in front of our window (on Belgrade Street), so it had become an integral part of our home life, just as a nice old piece of furniture. And at this time it lay there, in ruins.

However, we hadn't fallen into despair during those dark days of persecution, so we did not fall into despair at this time either. All over the city, as well as in our hearts, there was a breeze of hope. The terrible times were finally over and so a nice, new age was to come, and we would get over the difficulties somehow. [This attitude of hopefulness will be replaced with negativity later on.]

Borka immediately started to work again. She needed to rebuild her studio. It was impossible to get back into her old place where rain was falling through the roof, ruined by a bomb. So she did her work at a new place. She found a shop at 7 Terez Boulevard and she took everything that was left of her photography equipment: her Rolleiflex cameras, her magnifier, her development equipment, and her lamps. What more she needed, she carried there piece by piece as she could get what was available at those slowly opening shops. She carried everything herself, and two weeks after renting this studio she stood there, in her white working cloak, and photographed the Russian soldiers who were streaming in. It was amazing to see how those soldiers also felt the magic of her good motherly ways. "*Mamuska*" [a Hungarian word sounding like Russian, meaning dear old mummy] they told her, "we need a snapshot, me and this *tovaris* [Russian term for comrade] together, but we need it quickly as the day after tomorrow we leave for Berlin."

And Borka directed them, in her loving way, "You sit right here in this chair and please look here—no, not here, but a little bit up—now good!" She spoke to them in Hungarian as she only learned a few words in Russian later; however, she was still understood. Sons of every nation understand the language of love, goodness, and motherly caring. And Russians, especially so. And how gratefully they received their photos: "*Etot haraso*," "This is good," they said and brought her money, food, sugar, flour, many other things. Borka was active and happy, being herself, and took excellent care of the rest of us those days.

I didn't remain idle either. As soon as I more or less recovered from an illness that kept me in bed for a few weeks, due to a deficiency of vitamins that manifested itself in the slow healing of a minor leg injury, I began work as a Russian interpreter at Kende Zsiga's [Zsigmond Kende] place. I went to the city's Russian headquarters together with Zsiga and did my interpretation work.

Now it was fortunate for me that many years earlier, sometime in 1931 and then later in on in the 1930s, that I learned Russian. I translated what Zsiga told me and it was quite satisfactory that I then translated it into Pushkin's eloquent style. But when I had to translate the town commander's usually friendly but sometimes furious speeches into Hungarian, it was more difficult for me. It was difficult because I required time to become familiar with his dialect. However, we somehow succeeded together with Zsiga present, as well as at other places, when I went together with the other leaders of the Central Cooperative of Dairy Shops. I earned some money and also received some food that was brought from the countryside intended for their workmen and other colleagues.

Once, as I was sitting in Dairy Shops's office, an officer of the neighbouring Mauthner's Seed yard came in. When this official saw me interpreting, he asked me to translate a notice for him into Russian. Naturally I did it. "How much do I owe you?" he asked. "It is all right, you need not pay anything," I answered him. "But I hope you let me show our gratitude by giving you some food, won't you?" he asked me. "Obviously, thank you very much," was my answer. In a mere five minutes he returned, handing me a small sack full of beans, actually ten kilograms of beans! That meant great joy because that was enough for the entire family for fourteen days. I was happy to take it home to Borka. The beans were of a good quality and Borka prepared lovely soups and vegetable dishes with them.

Then I worked as an interpreter for my friend Monath who had a bakery and the Russians brought him flour in their trucks and he baked bread for them. Monath gave me a loaf of bread, weighing two kilograms, which was also extremely valuable to us and I also brought this home happily. I received bread, weighing one kilogram, as payment for a second morning's interpretation work. When the second lieutenant put the bread on the truck four women arrived with their babies in their arms. All of them received a loaf of bread weighing two kilograms each. Then the second lieutenant caught sight of me and certainly realised that I looked like someone who had been hungry for a long time. I lost 35 kilos in weight during the war. He directed one of his soldiers to give me a loaf of bread. I asked Monath if I could accept the bread and he answered and said that naturally I could. Again I happily brought the bread home.

But the next day I received the greatest gift. That day I worked for the lieutenant himself, counting how many kilograms of flour were used to bake how many kilograms of bread, and how much fuel was used. During our work together, I talked with the lieutenant who was a very educated man. At the end of our conversation he turned to Monath, and said, "Give the interpreter gentleman some loaves of bread, weighing ten kilograms." Nobody who did not live in those days can understand what this gesture meant to us: it meant happiness. I was careful with the bread and took home one two-kilogram loaf every two days. Because of my economical distribution, we were able to have bread for ten days!

After finishing the interpretations I also went to the Ganz factory to renew my contacts. I thought that those among my official colleagues who were fascists would be embarrassed to see me. I thought they would have a guilty conscience, would apologise, but would be nonetheless happy to see I had survived the war. What happened was quite different. One of my former friends, whom I considered to be the least sympathetic to fascism, expressed his happiness because of my escape but he told me the following, "Thank God you survived. It was a terrible time, almost all the Jews living in the country perished." "And this is a pity," he added, speaking as an expert, "as they were the better. It would have been better if the Jews of Pest would have been killed as there were many bad elements among them." I gazed at him. "Oh, I beg your pardon," he said. "I did not mean it this way. I know that you are also from Pest."

Next time I visited another friend. He mustn't have been a Nazi, I thought! And he even had some distinct Jewish roots, maybe one of his grandfathers. He turned to me in a somewhat friendly manner. "It was really awful," he said. "Those roguish Germans! You know, I have always disliked them!" (It was really true!) "But things are really bad now! Those times were not so bad. Of course, if we don't consider things against Jews."

I was astonished! If we don't consider? How is it possible not to consider 600,000 people being killed?!

This sudden insight to the inner life of Hungarian "middle class gentlemen" had an awful effect on me. Maybe it was also due to smoking too much, or to my two hour walk on foot through dirty, muddy streets with my leg still tied up with bandages. Actually, in my overall poor condition, I was unable to bear this shock, and so I fainted on the spot.

My friend was really frightened and ran to call a doctor. The doctor arrived and brought me to consciousness with some cognac. There was also another "friend" of mine in that room, I mean a colleague, who always had a friendly attitude towards me. He was in a subordinate position to my other friend of this story and so he turned to him in a servile way: "Why did you run away for a doctor yourself? It would have also been possible to send a junior officer!" So I received a final picture of the real nature of this "friend" of mine. He felt rank and title, the basis of all this feudal protectionist Hungary, to be beneath him, when his boss ran by himself away to call for a doctor to save my life. I still consider this man an honest and humane person and consider him to be my friend, and am grateful to him for saving my life when he got rapid help.

I don't put his name here and I didn't mention his name when telling this story to anyone either, except to Borka and Buba, so as not to wound his honour. I am convinced that basically he is a good and humane man. (There's a long history in Hungary of being afraid of the consequences of giving information, even in such private forums as one's personal diary or during an everyday chat with friends.) Nevertheless he was unable to recover immediately from being contaminated by Nazi ideas and propaganda for twenty-five years and he may have been reluctant to change. However, it is possible for him to heal and I think he has already started to heal. I have a bad opinion about the other gentleman.

I had to reassess my situation at the Ganz works. I did not want to work there again as salaries were so low (I would have received only US$2 or maximum $3 monthly and that wasn't worth it). I could earn a lot more money if I did translations on my own even considering the miserable income for intellectual work those days. I was offered the choice between a lump sum settlement and a half pension worth a civil servant pension. (I wasn't entitled to receive a full pension as I was not a member of the union.) I chose a lump sum settlement. One of my main motives to do so was that in this way my widow would receive 50% of my pension for ten years after my death. That will be good, I said. I never did even consider the possibility that I may be the one to be left a widower, a real orphan, since I'm eight years older than Borka. And Borka is the epitome of life.

I also asked that the Ganz works send translations to my home and I be paid as any other client. And so they did that. Once they even called me to come in and do an urgent job right on the spot. After completing the main portion of this job, I went outside to Kobanyai Road because I had to meet another client of mine, a Russian officer whose headquarters were close to the Ganz works. This officer was the commander of one of the so-called "*trofejnaja*" (Russian for boot) brigades.

On my way back to the factory, three more gentlemen, delegates of the Yugoslavian government, and I were stopped by a Russian soldier, who looked very angry. "*Davaj*! Go! Work! Push the car!" The three Yugoslavian gentlemen just laughed as they considered what was happening to be humorous. They didn't mind pushing a car for an hour. However, I had to return to the Ganz works factory as I still had some work to finish. So I tried to explain to the Russian soldier that there was no point in my pushing a car for Ganz as Ganz needed me to work as an engineer.

I was lucky to make a grammatical mistake when explaining this, saying the simpler form, "I'm engineer Ganz" instead of "I'm an engineer at Ganz", "*Ja inzsener Ganza*". In fact the Russian really thought I was the engineer Ganz for whom the factory was named.

So he stopped and saluted me. "Oh so, you are Engineer Ganz. I beg your pardon. Of course you may go away." And so a grammatical mistake saved me from an hour of car pushing. The Russian military commander of the Ganz works, whom I told right on the spot what just happened, was amazed by this story. [It was quite common at the end of the war for Soviet soldiers to stop people in the street, man or woman, young or old, healthy or sick, to do some urgent work. This work was either digging graves or cleaning up the ruins of buildings or anything else needed. In fact, many people were taken away to the Soviet Union for days, weeks, or even years.]

Soon after this episode I began another important project. An engineer at Ganz, an old colleague of mine, who also escaped death during the war in an incredible way, got some work for me to translate from the Hungarian Electric Works. I translated from German into Russian every contract of the Matravidek Power Plant. It meant a great amount of work that must be done swiftly: some 100,000 words a month if I remember correctly. Nevertheless, I was paid quite poorly as I received only one filler [Hungarian for penny] per word. Still, it meant twenty dollars at the beginning and later forty dollars per month. In the project's early stages I employed only one typist to help me, and later I employed two, one in the morning and one in the afternoon.

Later, or precisely sometime in June 1945, I also received important work from the English. These projects paid better; however, compared to the income needed to meet our needs, also bad. For my first great project, the translation of Russian restitution transport records to English, I was paid in Hungarian pengos [Hungarian currency between 1927 and 1946; due to extreme monetary inflation, it was later replaced by the korona and then by the forint; the pengo was subdivided into 100 fillers] equalling £15. I subsequently received many smaller scale works: one for £2, one for £3, one for £7. Every time I received my payment for these works, I happily rushed to Borka's studio to hand her my salary. Her blissful smile was reward enough for all my efforts. These times, and also on some other occasions, we went to an espresso bar named Mocca that was next to Borka's studio to have a cup of coffee together. How happy these moments were for us! We sat there together as if we were a young couple falling in love or as two students who can only meet secretly in a cafe and are blissful to see each other. Although we also spent our late afternoons and evenings together, I never missed this morning rendezvous at that espresso bar if there was any way to do so. Waitresses already knew and loved Borka so when they learned the awful news at the end of August 1946, they cried. And so did people all along Terez Boulevard: colleagues in her studio, the neighbouring hairdressers, everybody cried.

Buba also had some income and was first employed by MABI (Association of Hungarian Insurance Companies) as an insurance mathematician and later by the Peasant Association as a statistician. Income for the three of us, the main portion earned by Borka, covered our daily needs. However, it was not enough to rebuild our home that was sacked and ruined. [In the long run, the family did not return there to live.] Borka's deepest desire, if at all possible, was to rebuild our home, which she had guarded so faithfully and thoroughly, in its original, intact state. Our friends comforted us: Borka should not worry as she had five sisters and brothers, all of them were living in more or less favourable conditions, especially two of them, Feri and Lilly, both of whom had become incredibly rich. Feri's [Dr Franz Alexander] fixed yearly income was US$24,000 in 1936. [There is no data to say where Artur got this figure. In fact, Feri's income was probably much higher inasmuch as he offered his daughter Silvia's estranged husband, Dr George Rotariu, a sum of $50,000 to remove himself from the life of his infant daughter, Ilonka, editor of this book]. And, as a psychoanalyst, he received $50 for an hour of analysis [actually, here again, Artur underestimated the hourly fee]. He already owned a big "ranch" [a summer home in La Jolla] in California. And then there was Lilly, who was also extremely rich and whose husband was mentioned as one of the richest New York millionaires. They wouldn't even feel any financial effect if they helped their sister! If only they could send us three days' income it would have been enough for us to establish our new home. We didn't even count the three other sisters and brother as ones who might help us.

It was still impossible for us to send a letter from Budapest to the USA, however from Romania it would work. Peter [probably Kende Peter] planned to travel to Bucharest for a few months and we asked him to write to Feri about our situation. He really did. A couple of months later we received a telegraph from Feri: "Received Peter's report, you will hear from me as soon as possible." His telegraph made us feel very happy. So, as soon as the postal transport was operating again, we will hear from him, and he will send us some financial help. We tried to figure out how much he would send. $1,000? We would even have been satisfied with $500 as we thought Lilly to be at least four times richer than him. So, if she also sent money using this rationale and ratio, it would have been enough to establish a new home. A couple of weeks later the postal transport began to operate and we received the long-awaited money transfer from Feri. He sent $25—which might have been half his hourly fee.

In the meantime, we also connected with Lilly. I still have Borka's draft letter written in her beautiful handwriting. I translated it into English so that the Hungarian text did not alert the censors and delay delivery. This letter would have even moved a rock. Every word of hers was correct and true and full of love and trust. Certainly this time Lilly would also do her utmost to return all that love that Borka had shown towards her, her entire life. We received Lilly's reply: she transferred $50 instead of the $2,000 that we had hoped for.

Borka replied kindly that we were grateful for her tiny but rapid help, it was good that we could buy some food with it, and now we were waiting for her real help. The messenger arrived again and brought us, instead of the real help that we hoped, again only fifty dollars. We were speechless.

Meanwhile Erzsi also contacted us. We never counted on her for any help as we knew that she made her living entirely on her own. She was a working woman without extra income. But, Erzsi sent us $40 and an additional $40 later on and that meant more to us than if we had received $4,000 from Lilly. She also sent us many packages of items, selected with care and love: perfect clothes, food, and other things. We had expected more or less nothing from her and yet she helped us the most.

Feri and Lilly's apparent callousness also astonished Erzsi who wrote to Borka, saying that both Feri and Lilly became quite rich and it appeared that their great wealth and property had a bad effect on their personal character. She was so shocked by Lilly sending us only $50 the second time she sent money: Erzsi sent $20 from her own limited income and also insisted that Feri send us $15 more. She handed the $35 to Lilly to send it for us via the consul. It was only when the messenger arrived and we claimed the $35, we learned of Erzsi's letter. However, it turned out that the consul did not receive the money. This happened during the spring of 1946. The money finally arrived from Lilly at the very beginning of September, 1946, ten days after the catastrophe.

I think that Lilly obviously forgot to send us the money that Erzsi gave her. Later, at the end of August, when she learned by telegraph of the catastrophe, she recalled this tiny memory lapse. So, at that time she reimbursed the money. Ten days after Borka's death.

The first sign of life we received from America came from Mrs Stricker, Mausi Polanyi. She said she sent us seven packages: two from Erzsi and five from Mausi; two of which were intended for us and three for others. We were so happy with the news in this telegraph. There were miners stuck in a mine after a collapse, suffering, and finally they heard the jingling sound of rescuing hammers from the other side of the bedrock. Unfortunately the miners did not survive and we were only able to hand the packages to their loved ones.

Meanwhile we received very, very sad news: Edith, Erzsi's daughter, died in September 1945. Borka wept for her from the bottom of her heart as she loved Edith very much and I also had only pleasant memories of her cheerful lovely nature. Unfortunately she had diabetes and died suddenly during an operation. Erzsi hasn't been able to find comfort anywhere as all sense and purpose disappeared from her life. Poor Erzsi.

What was especially hurtful to both of us was that Lilly didn't even find it necessary to reply to Borka's deeply moving letter. No, not even the rich should act this way. Well, she sent some

I have just found a letter from Borka, sent to me from Italy in 1937, when I had to delay my travel to join her by four weeks due to my demanding work at the Ganz works. When I wasn't able to bear missing her any longer, I called her on the phone and told her how dreadfully I missed her and that I only called to hear her voice. She was moved by my love and she put down these sentiments in her letter to me:

My Sweetheart,

I was really worried yesterday evening, when you called me! And this long time to wait! My dear! I am so sorry, that you are so unwell and that these last couple of days were so hard for you! Earlier I considered the distanced voice of your letters meaning that those times are over, when my being away was so difficult for you, and I admit that it made me feel somewhat bad—, while on the other hand I was happy that this can be easier for you now. But now I can see, that you still need your old Borax. I don't deny being a little bit proud. However, this feeling is suppressed by the pain of your feeling so bad now. Well, my dear, this would be over really so soon. You will be here with us in a couple of days and will enjoy it so much! The first time when you didn't arrive when agreed I was waiting for you so eagerly that I can't find words to describe!

I was very sad about your delay. And thought you even didn't mind that you couldn't come earlier and that may be better this way! But now I am waiting for you very much again and this time it won't be long! It may be better that you travel directly here without stopping anywhere! And you can have a rest here! So we can save a whole day. …

Please be clever and patient as we will be happily together only a few days from now.

With hot hugs from your Borax.

She wrote this on 20 July 1937.

A couple of days earlier, 14 July 1937, she wrote this to me:

My sweetheart,

Thank you for your letter. I'm sorry for that my friends neglect you. Renee is nasty, please tell her that she should really spend some time with you.

We are still very well. Buba already looks great and I can feel so well and natural as I haven't felt for long. Now we have a calm life here but by the time you arrive it will be more stirring as we will be more here. Buba has already got to know two girls. We often go to a cinema here in the evenings, it is rather cheap, only 2 liras and of course it's so pleasantly situated outdoors. Today I was at Forte at the weekly fair. It was really very nice. Forte is a nice bathing resort but our small place is even more pleasant. Please go to Guttmann's to buy yourself a pair of trousers made of linen. It is very important! It should be broad enough and it shouldn't be white. You will obviously need it here. We are also looking for the cake very much. I will write you in my next week's letter what you will need to carry here. … Please start your way here immediately as soon as possible. I am waiting for you so much!

Thousands of kisses from your Borax.

So how should I bear that this Borax is not any more here on earth?

I should also write about her diary where I can see all the sadness this warm-hearted little girl suffered from being unloved by her sisters and brothers and the history of her childhood loves. And I also should put here her year 1929 note in her diary about our marriage. Nevertheless, I should do it some other time as now it saps my energy. Now I can only cry, cry.

I get back to my own story. Now it is winter of 1945. We celebrate Christmas in spite of harsh conditions and we are quite happy. Those happy Christmas Eves that Borka created! This day was a real celebration with her as it meant togetherness, happiness, and love! These twenty-six years were all like Christmas for me, to be together with her and all these years she was my present! She herself was the angel from heaven, she herself was the little Jesus [referring to the text of an old Hungarian Christmas song and Christmas-related phrases], how miraculous her celebrations were! We also had many other celebrations besides Christmas on our family calendar such as her birthday, 27 July. And she never forgot 6 April, my birthday either, so she invited a company to see me. Nevertheless, being with her was a celebration in and of itself. But from now on I only have weekdays. My only celebration now, yet a painful one, is when I have a chance to sink into my memories of her for but an hour.

Writing is becoming more and more difficult for me as we approach the time of the actual catastrophe. It was easier, of course only relatively, as I also felt my tears of pain, when I only wrote about all that pleasure that she gave me just by being alive. But it is so difficult to put down that one thing which caused me endless pain, when she left this earthly life. It seems to me that this is my price to pay for happiness. The nicer it all was, the better it all was, the more awful it is, now that it is all over.

I still have to put down that a great pleasure took place at the end of Borka's life when Buba got married. Borka was happy to see that Buba found happiness in his life and she loved Kato. She could see how much Buba loved her and how much Kato has loved him. The marriage took place in January of 1946. A common friend of the young couple, who has become a prefect in the new regime, led the ceremony at Budapest 5th District Prefecture at Honved Street. We had lunch at Kato's mother's who had a dinner for us after the ceremony. I have to be grateful that Borka had this chance to see Buba happy. The young couple dwelled here at our tiny place and Borka took care of them and made them feel as good as possible every day. Kato also loved Borka very much.

Our dear Borka, who was as good as an angel, was happy to be given a new child besides her two old ones: me and Buba. Things also turned good at our jobs as well. We were even able to struggle with awful inflation: we collected adopengos, that money of our new temporary currency [that was valid between January and July 1946] and Borka always took our money to the bank herself to exchange herself. At the end of this period we had 12 million adopengos. When our acquaintance from London, Mrs Foster, an officer at the BBC, sent us that four and a half pounds that she owed me, after exchanging it I brought some 4 yotta million [= 1,000,000,000,000,000,000,000,000 = 10 to the power of 24] adopengos to Borka at the shop. And she was even happy with this.

However, Borka had experienced some problems in her health condition since spring. Her blood pressure got even higher, so high that the doctor did not want us to know. She was treated by Doctor Flamm and received injections to lower her blood pressure, and also from Renee, who also visited her in her studio in the mornings. And these injections really worked and her blood pressure was stabilised within a few weeks' time. I recall that she got three such courses: forty injections first and later twenty and thirty. We considered her high blood pressure a minor problem that could happen to anyone. I never did suspect that it might lead to a catastrophe. I was awfully reproachful to myself after the catastrophe: why had I considered this problem in such an easy-going way? If only we had forced Borka to stay in bed immediately, if only we had insisted she mustn't work anymore, if only we had forced her to rest, only lie in her bed; could we have saved her from the catastrophe somehow? Lilly Hajdu, as well as Renee and especially Doctor Flamm all agreed that it all would have been completely useless. It would even have been impossible, as she wouldn't have let us do so, she wouldn't have borne not doing anything. Lilly Hajdu said, if we forced her to stay inactive, she would have died even earlier. She would have become miserable and would have become awfully agitated, and that would have brought on the catastrophe even sooner. It would have been impossible to do so, even had we suspected the catastrophe. However, we hadn't.

And later there was her plan to travel to Switzerland. Magda wrote to Borka and invited her to Arosa, Switzerland for two weeks. Erzsi and Lilly would also be there. Borka was extremely happy with this plan. That she had a chance to meet her sisters again, whom—in spite of everything and forgiving them everything—she loved so much. Nevertheless, I tried to argue against this plan. "Arosa is 1,800 metres above sea level, my Borax," I told her. "This is not for you. You remember what the doctor in Abbazia told us, do you? You mustn't go above 1,000 metres, considering this high blood pressure of yours." "We will get over this problem somehow," she said. "I will find accommodations somewhere in the village, a lower altitude, under the mountain, and my sisters will come there to see me." I didn't rely on this plan, as people usually don't keep to these kinds of things. Of course I didn't even suspect what kind of catastrophe all this could lead to; nevertheless, I knew that real danger is a brain stroke that may lead to some paralysis. I tried to dissuade Borka from her plan but she was adamant. She was especially happy with the prospect of meeting up with Lilly. "When we get face to face with Lilly," she said, "I can even melt her heart of stone." Poor Borka! What a bad disappointment would have waited for her there! *Lilly didn't even travel to Arosa!*

It took us much ado to get a visa and the Russian travel permit for Borka. We went to the Russian embassy on Bajza Street to get this paperwork and Jeno Varga also made an offer to assist her, but nothing worked. She didn't receive the Russian travel permit.

If we can even talk of any good luck after such an awful misfortune, the lack of a Russian travel permit for Borka was actually a real blessing in disguise. As the following weeks would prove, if she had travelled, getting tired from her train trip, as well being excited about her journey, it could have led to the catastrophe then, even without the effect of altitude in Arosa. It may have happened already in her railway car in Vienna. And this way she would have not been surrounded by us; she would have been alone and away from home when death came.

On Wednesday, the 14th of August, Borka woke me up at half past three in the morning to tell me she was feeling terribly bad. I sprang up to wake up Buba who could run faster than me and sent him to get Dr Pilis who lived on the first floor of our building. Doctor Pilis came up here within five minutes and gave Borka an injection. She got another one at half past five am and that time her pain was lessening. Doctor Flamm arrived here by eight and said that it would be better to take Borka to the hospital for a medical check-up. I asked him not to do so as I was fearful Borka would become more agitated in the hospital and hoped she could recover at home. Doctor Flamm agreed to wait until the next day and in the hopes she would better. But she didn't get better. On Thursday morning Buba and Kato took her to the Uzsoki Street Hospital by car. There 500 ml of blood was drawn and she received a 1,000 ml saline solution injection. That time she got better, again, but the next morning she had a brain stroke and by the time I arrived in the afternoon she was unconscious. Doctor Flamm told me that her condition was critical but not hopeless. If her unconsciousness lasted less than three days it would mean that bleeding was absorbed and she would recover. I held onto this hope with all my being and was really unable to think of any other outcome than recovery. Sunday morning I noticed with extreme happiness that her mind was clearer. She said a few words. She said

"Thank you" to the nurse. And later she said, "Please give me a dram of water." And when the nurse did so very carefully (it had to be done with much care so that the water did not get into her windpipe instead of her throat), then she told her in her sweet voice "This was not a whole dram," so she was given some more. In these few words I saw a sign of her recovery. I was so happy that I gave 100 forints to both nurses asking them to take care of her as if their own. She was somewhat clearer by Monday noon but it was all over by Tuesday. Doctor Flamm also called in another specialist, a neurologist from the Jewish hospital, as it is expected in his field of practice, and however, I think it was all in vain. His reason to do so was to see whether there was some other problem and it would be possible to help. But there was no other problem. It was simply a stroke and it was impossible to help. We stayed with her all day, Tuesday and Wednesday. The doctors' reports worsened and were pessimistic but still left some hope. I didn't give up hope for a single minute. But it was all futile. On Thursday, 22 August at 4 pm the catastrophe took place. The heart of the best woman, the best wife, the best mother, the best daughter, the best sister, the best friend, the best mate stopped beating. She, who meant life and all the world to me was no longer alive. I fell down to hug her and kissed her dear lips one last time.

We buried her in the morning on Monday, the 26th of August. Hajdu Lilly said a farewell to her in the name of all her girlfriends. She said, Buba always called Borka Motherheart, and that's what she really was.

We all lost a mother when we lost her, but I lost much more. My happiness, my life. We all cried and we all felt that awful loss. But over the loss of all of us, the most awful thing is, that she herself no longer exists.

I am unable to write any more.

This is the end.

AFTERWORD

Artur Renyi died in Budapest in 1950 when he was hit by a car while walking down from Svabhegy, a hill on the Buda side of the Danube. No one knows if the accident occurred because of his absent-mindedness, not noticing the approaching car, or because of another reason. What is known is that Artur was devastated when his wife died as can be deduced from the abrupt ending of his memoir.

His son Alfred Renyi (20 March 1921–1 February 1970) was a brilliant Hungarian mathematician who made contributions in many areas of that field and is most known for his probability theory work. Institutes are named for him in Hungary. He was a member of the Hungarian Academy of Sciences and, like his mother, died prematurely. He had one child, Zsuzsi Renyi, who translated this memoir along with her daughter, Nauszika Mathe-Arvay.

ABOUT THE EDITORS

Ilonka Venier Alexander is a clinical social worker and the granddaughter of Dr Franz Alexander, the founder of the Chicago Institute for Psychoanalysis and considered by many to be the most important American analyst of the 20th century as well as the father of psychosomatic medicine. Ilonka wrote a biography of her grandfather in 2015, *The Life and Times of Franz Alexander: From Budapest to California*, and has written another forthcoming book about growing up with Franz Alexander. She lives in Nova Scotia with her husband and five cats, and is a host parent to international high school students. Hobbies include photography, travel, philatelics, and community advocacy. She is a board member of the local chapter of the Canadian Mental Health Association.

Nauszika Mathe-Arvay was born in Budapest in 1973 and still lives in the neighbourhood. In the last decade she has worked as a psychologist for an elementary school. She is especially interested in how to create an integrative community in which every member can play a valuable role. She applies narrative methods, restorative practice and anti-bullying ideas. She considers all personal, family and community roots as well as intercultural aspects very important.

Zsuzsanna Renyi worked as a historian for the Hungarian Academy's Research Institute and was a lecturer for ELTE

University in Budapest. She is retired but now works as a translator and English teacher. She is especially interested in Anglo-American cultural history and civilization. In recent years she has published a book of interviews about her father, the mathematician Alfred Renyi. She is enjoying family life and her grandchildren.

Made in the USA
Monee, IL
04 November 2026

67381836R10085